Techniques for
Personal Grow
by
Muriel
Schiffman

SELF
THERAPY

Illustrated by Jessica Wilhelm
Cover Design by Michael Patrick Cronan
Originally published by Self Therapy Press
Wingbow Press books are published and distributed
by Bookpeople
2940 Seventh Street, Berkeley, California 94710

Library of Congress Catalog Card Number: 73-75227
ISBN 0-914640-01-1
Tenth Printing, September 1982

To

Bernie with love.

ACKNOWLEDGMENTS

I WANT to thank the many students throughout these teaching years who generously shared with me their own experiments in self therapy and gave me confidence that it can be taught.

I am most grateful to my Good Listeners who helped clarify my thinking: Lucy, Germaine, and especially Hilda.

The following people gave me encouragement when I needed it: Robert Spitzer, M.D. and James Terrill, Ph.D., Mental Research Institute, Palo Alto and Abraham Maslow, Ph.D., Brandeis University.

I am deeply indebted to Anthony Sutich, Psychotherapist, Editor of THE JOURNAL OF HUMANISTIC PSYCHOLOGY for his guidance and for his faith in my work.

Menlo Park, California
March 1967

Except for members of my family and certain intimate friends, persons mentioned in this book are not actual individuals, but composites of several different people.

CONTENTS

INTRODUCTION

THIS BOOK describes certain self help techniques I have been teaching for more than one decade and practicing for two. Psychotherapists in the community tell me that my lectures have helped students to recognize when they needed professional help, taught them how to get their money's worth from psychotherapy and speed up the process, and provided them with tools to continue the therapeutic work on their own after completing psychotherapy.

I have been happy to learn this, but in the main my lectures are designed for the so-called "normal" person in our culture: that is, those with mildly neurotic tendencies, people like myself who may never need professional help. Shadows of the past sometimes contaminate the present and narrow down the future for all of us. The purpose of my self therapy techniques is to confront the past and put it in its place. Only then are we released to live the present more fully and grow into a richer future, able to use more of our true potential.

SUFFERING CAN BE THERAPEUTIC

MANY YEARS ago I was cooped up in a small city apartment with a two-year-old who wanted Mommy to talk to her, sing to her, play with her. But every once in a while I would have one of those days when I plodded through my chores mechanically, longing only to lie down in a darkened room and be left alone. In former years I could disguise that recurrent depression with a little extra lipstick and a bright, false smile; but these tactics were not reassuring to my little girl. A talkative, lively mother who suddenly shuts herself off is a rejecting mother. My blue days made her anxious and demanding, unable to settle down with her toys.

The morning after one of these bad days I watched Jeanie respond to my renewed warmth like a flower unfolding in the sun and remembered how troubled she had been yesterday. I told myself I could not continue to expose her to my recurring depressions. What kind of damage were these moods doing to her? My own childhood had been so unhappy I longed to give her the security and stability I had missed. I had to cure myself of that neurotic symptom.

We had no money for professional psychiatric help then. If there were low-cost clinics in those days I had never heard of them. So I rushed in where angels fear to tread; with the courage born of desperation and naïveté, I began to use myself as a guinea pig in a fumbling attempt at self therapy.

I did a lot of foolish things which I now know are a waste of time, but I stumbled on the key to self therapy: I learned to *feel painful emotions* I had been avoiding all my life. I explored attitudes and relationships that forced me to feel rage and grief and anxiety, and I did a great deal of crying. For two long years I unearthed a hidden part of my life, and suffered and then it suddenly dawned on me that my old, recurrent depression was gone. Somewhere along the way I had lost it, and it has never come back.

What began as a clumsy, desperate attempt to climb out of an abyss has now become a way of life. Self therapy has cured me of a cat phobia, fear of driving, peptic ulcer symptom, and has given

1

me a measure of control over my compulsive eating and headaches. But more important, it has brought me new spontaneity in my relations with the people I love (I no longer run to the child guidance books with every new problem), and a new freedom to explore my own potential as a human being. Life is richer and more satisfying —I am never bored.

"Isn't it dangerous to analyze yourself?" people ask. I do not teach self analysis (how to understand your basic personality problems, how to change your character), but merely self therapy, a means of utilizing your awareness of the foolish thing you did yesterday and today, a way of discovering why you did it so you can avoid doing it tomorrow.

"Isn't introspection dangerous?" Introspection may indeed be a danger signal. Obsessive preoccupation with your faults, too much soul-searching (What's the matter with me?), continual feelings of guilt or shame or inadequacy are all clues that you need professional help. Self therapy avoids such generalizations as, "What kind of a neurotic am I?" It teaches you to stop intellectualizing about yourself in an abstract way, stop thinking of yourself as a case history, and begin to feel your genuine emotions. It is just the opposite of introspection.

SELF-DEFEATING BEHAVIOR

"WHY DID I feel like crying? I know he didn't mean to hurt me."

"Why did I lose my temper? She's only a child!"

"How could I make such a fool of myself?"

"I should never have said those cruel words."

Sound familiar? The normal person is rational most of the time but every once in a while he looks back and wonders, "What made me do that?" Each of us has certain blind spots where we are not free to use our own intelligence and experience to solve a problem. Every time we get stuck in one of our vulnerable areas, we tend to act in self-defeating ways. By that I mean if you want approval you will get disapproval, if you need love from a person you will force him to reject you, if you are trying to build up your self-respect you will make a fool of yourself.

When do you act in a self-defeating way? When something comes up that threatens to make you feel a "forbidden" emotion, an emotion you once thought was too dangerous to feel. Suppose your mother frustrated you in some special way when you were very small. You were tempted to hate her, but hate seemed too dangerous (she might stop loving you; or your hate might have magic power to destroy her; etc.). Now you are grown up and some motherly person frustrates you in a similar way. You are actually no longer weak and helpless, nor is this your mother (even if she is your mother, she is no longer the powerful person on whom you are dependent), but the child within you reacts in the same old way. That child cannot see the changes time has wrought. It distorts the picture to fit the same old scene; misinterprets the other's expression, tone, words. You are faced with a situation that looks something like an earlier one where you dared not feel hate, and you act as if that feeling is still too dangerous. As soon as you are tempted to feel that forbidden emotion you quickly cover it up with something else: another, fake emotion.

All this happens without any awareness on your part. You do not recognize the scene as familiar, you do not notice the forbidden feel-

3

ing threatening to pop out. All you actually feel is the pseudo-emotion used to cover up the hidden feeling.

What feelings do we hide from ourselves? Any kind. What feelings do we use as covers? Also, any kind. Anger can cover fear, and fear can cover anger. Guilt, shame, fear, anxiety, hate, rage, love: any human emotion can be hidden, or used to disguise a hidden feeling. Furthermore, (and this makes it more confusing) a pseudo-emotion feels just like a genuine emotion: fake anger feels exactly like real anger.

What happens when you are busy covering up a hidden feeling with a false one? You cannot see things clearly; you distort and misinterpret reality. You are not free to use your intelligence and experience to solve a problem. Whenever you hide an emotion from yourself, you tend to handle a problem in an automatic, stereotyped manner; you use the same old self-defeating method that did not work the first time and which you have been blindly repeating ever since. The child within you never had a chance to experiment and learn a better way; in this area you have not grown up. not made use of knowledge and experience that belong to your grown-up self.

Suppose you learn to peel away the layer of that apparent feeling. that fake cover-emotion. and dare to feel what lies hidden just underneath? You can then throw away that useless old cover which has been misleading you all these years. You do not have to act in that compulsively blind, self-defeating way any more. It is as if you had been wearing crooked, distorting glasses and now you straighten them out. Lo and behold, you can see the whole situation is a different light; you recognize people as their own unique selves instead of mere shadows from your own past; you hear what they are really saying instead of misinterpreting their words. You are finally free to use your intelligence and experience to experiment with new ways of solving problems. This does not guarantee that you will solve all problems perfectly, (some problems are insoluble) but this time; if things go wrong you can try to figure out what happened, instead of passing the buck, blaming the other fellow or Fate for your misfortune. You can now learn from experience, in this area, just as you normally do in other, undamaged areas.

By this time you are probably asking two questions: 1. If the fake, cover emotion feels just like a genuine one, how can I tell when it is real or not? 2. If I know it is only a cover, what can I do about it? This book will attempt to answer both those questions.

4

I cannot promise that you will discover your Basic Neurosis or the Real You or anything so ambitious. Self therapy is simply a tool for day-by-day living, a way of being more honest with yourself, a technique for using your intelligence and experience in damaged areas as well as you do in situations where you have nothing to hide from yourself. You know how you function when you are feeling safe and comfortable with yourself, not needing to kid yourself. Self therapy will help you do as well as that in spots where up until now you have been acting blindly, automatically. It will help you be more like yourself, like the person you are when you have your wits about you.

Self therapy makes use of each day's failures; nothing need be wasted; all is grist that comes to your mill. It is a way to live more productively here and now rather than wait until you have "cured" your neurosis. I can feel like a neurotic and act like a healthy person; I can feel like a child and act like an adult.

HOW TO FEEL A HIDDEN EMOTION

I HAVE OUTLINED below five steps in the search for a hidden emotion. The whole process may take minutes or months, the time lapse between steps may be uneven, and you may move backward or forward sometimes.

Step 1. *Recognize an inappropriate reaction.* You notice yourself reacting to some situation in a manner your intellect tells you is not appropriate (Why do I feel so sad? He doesn't mean to hurt me.) Since any emotion can be used to cover another, and the fake emotion feels just as real as a genuine, appropriate one, it is difficult to recognize an inappropriate reaction while it is going on if you are a beginner in self therapy. This kind of self-awareness is easier when you are looking back, after it is all over (I wonder why I was so angry yesterday; she's only a little girl!) Depression, anxiety, obsessive thinking can all be called inappropriate reactions. They are not definite emotions. They are always covers for something you are afraid to feel. Tension, headache, physical symptoms of anxiety (trouble breathing, heart pounding) are all clues that you are hiding something from yourself.

Step 2. *Feel the apparent emotion.* Sometimes you deliberately try to avoid an inappropriate reaction (It's silly to be hurt; he doesn't mean it.), but you must feel that emotion, no matter how irrational it seems. There is no short cut to the unconscious; you cannot feel a hidden emotion unless you begin with the apparent emotion which covers it.

Sometimes the apparent emotion seems dangerous (So furious I could kill her—but she's only a baby!) You do not have to act out your inappropriate feelings. Thoughts and actions are not identical, they can be separated; your feelings have no magic powers. You can always take your apparent emotion elsewhere. Talk about it to someone else, write it out, feel it. But do not swallow it down.

If you are trying to explore yesterday's inappropriate reaction warm up that cooled-off emotion by talking about it to a good listener. Suppose you are tracking down the hidden feeling behind a head-

6

ache. You will have to be a detective and work backward, looking for clues. When did this symptom begin? What happened then? How did I feel?

Step 3. *What else did I feel?* Just before the apparent feeling, what other feeling did you have? Not a hidden emotion, but one you felt for a brief moment and paid little attention to; one which was drowned out as soon as the apparent emotion took over. If you try, you can remember it, just as you can recall something you saw out of the corner of your eye, hardly realizing at the time you were seeing it. For instance, maybe you felt a pang of fear just before the apparent feeling, anger, developed.

Step 4. *What does this remind me of?* When have you reacted this way to a similar situation? What does this make you think of? Have you ever before noticed that you have some peculiar attitudes toward this kind of problem?

If this does not bring forth a hidden feeling, ask yourself, *What do I seem to be doing?* For a moment, take an objective view. If you were an outsider observing your behavior in this situation, what would it *look* as if you were doing?

In this step, (4), your intellect is asking questions, trying to get a rise out of your emotions. You are not looking for an intellectual explanation for your inappropriate reaction; you are not trying to explain the motives for your self-defeating behavior; you are not your own psychotherapist. You are merely trying to *feel* a hidden emotion. Keep trying different ideas until one of them evokes a strong emotion.

How do you know when you are feeling, not just thinking? What is the difference between an emotion and an intellectual idea? When you feel an emotion, you always feel some *physical* change. Your heart pounds or your breathing quickens, you may turn cold or begin to perspire, sometimes you feel shaky. The body always takes part in the emotion.

How do you know when you are feeling a *hidden* emotion? a) It is as intense as the apparent emotion you began with, if not more so. b) It displaces the apparent emotion. The feeling you began with is gone; it is merely an unimportant thought now.

Step 5. *Look for the pattern.* Do not look for your basic personality pattern, or anything so broad. Just try to find out what happened here. Now that you have felt your hidden emotion, you will probably remember other times when you were tempted to feel that forbidden feeling (without realizing it) and covered it up with this very same apparent emotion. You can be pretty sure that this will happen again. You are rarely "cured" of a hidden feeling just because you once felt it. Chances are, it will continue to lie in wait for you.

But now you are predictable to yourself. Next time you are faced with a similar problem, if you can remember this hidden feeling (you may not have to feel it again) you can discard that old cover, the apparent emotion. You will be free to experiment with a new way of handling the problem. For the first time in your life, in this kind of situation, you need not act in the old, automatic, self-defeating way. Now that you know your pattern (the tendency to cover this particular hidden feeling with this apparent feeling under this special kind of circumstance) you are free to use your intelligence and experience to act at least as wisely as in those undamaged areas where you never had to hide anything from yourself.

Sometimes you will forget what you have just learned, and find yourself reacting in the old way, covering up that hidden feeling once again with the same old fake feeling. But this time you will begin to look for the hidden feeling sooner (because you will notice the inappropriate reaction sooner) and find it more easily than before. Relearning is easier than learning. Each time this happens, the whole process will be speeded up, until eventually you will remember the hidden feeling *before* the apparent feeling (inappropriate reaction) is in full swing.

There are four paths to the hidden feeling: a) talking it out, b) thinking it through by yourself, c) writing it out, and d) "sneaking up" on the hidden feeling. I will describe all four of these methods in the following chapters, and illustrate them with anecdotes from my own experiences in self therapy.

8

THINKING OUT LOUD

ONE WAY to track down a hidden feeling is to talk it out in the presence of a good listener. What are the characteristics of a good listener? He is unshockable; he can comfortably accept all your "bad" feelings. He respects you as a fellow being and does not look down on you because you have problems; he cares about your suffering and tries to understand how you feel. A good listener (unless he is a professional helper) should not be personally involved in the particular problem you are trying to solve. Do not expect your husband, for instance, to help you find your hidden feelings about *him*. ("I hate you right now, darling, but I know it's only a cover for something else.") Only your psychotherapist can take this kind of brutal frankness.

Self therapy is the safest therapy in the world because each person, according to Karen Horney, has a built-in self-protective mechanism that keeps him from uncovering any emotion he is not yet strong enough to feel. But it is dangerous to have someone else push you into feeling something before you are ready. This means a non-professional helper must not interpret for you; he must not say anything which will force you to feel a hidden emotion before you discover it by yourself. A good listener, if he is not a professional helper, must be able to keep quiet and listen. Try to find someone who knows no more about psychology than you do, preferably less; then, if he is occasionally tempted to tell you what your hidden feeling is, you will be able to ignore his comments and remind him that you are just thinking out loud and need to work this through for yourself, and by yourself. ("Shut up and listen.")

The thinking-out-loud method is especially useful when you are trying to explore yesterday's inappropriate reaction; when you need to warm up that cooled-off apparent emotion. It is easier to re-live an experience when you describe it to someone else.

Example: One day I was washing dishes and listening to a Dixieland jazz record when an overwhelming desire to dance hit me. I peeped hopefully into the living-room, but Bernie was stretched out on the sofa looking exhausted, so I did not dare say a word, I tried thought control: I concentrated, I *willed* him to suggest dancing. My dear husband opened his eyes, stretched, stood up. My heart pounded. He went outside to do a little gardening. I could have killed him. (He doesn't deserve a wife like me; how can he be so insensitive; I always go sailing for his sake; he begrudges me a simple pleasure, etc. etc.). Then I tried dancing all by myself in the kitchen, but it turned into a dance of vengeance (Who needs you? I can dance alone.) and made me angrier, so I went back to the dishpan to suffer in silence.

After a while, the adult part of me woke up: Bernie doesn't know I'm dying to dance. I haven't told him. Why am I so angry? Little by little the anger died down, but it left me cranky and troubled. I had been through all this before, the craving to dance, the frustration, the anger. But this time it dawned on me that there was something peculiar about the whole thing. This was Step 1. *Notice an inappropriate reaction.*

I could not get any further by myself, so the next morning I visited a friend who has proven herself a good listener. I have often been a good listener for her too, so I did not feel I was exploiting her. It is a good idea to make use of different listeners from time to time. They get tired. Only a professional helper can comfortably bear the burden of *all* your problems.

My friend poured coffee and before I knew it, we were having a cozy visit and I had forgotten the purpose of this call. Watch for this: once your apparent emotion has cooled off you have a tendency to let sleeping dogs lie, but you cannot afford to waste good material for self therapy. I forced myself to cut the social chit-chat and get to work. Briefly I described my problem. Yesterday I had reached Step 1. Recognize an inappropriate reaction. It was foolish to be angry with Bernie; he didn't know I wanted to dance. Besides, this had happened too many times.

Step 2. *Feel apparent emotion.* That anger was dead and gone now. I described the scene in detail and let myself re-live it until I was angry again. When the anger was as intense as I could get it, I went on to

Step 3. *What else did I feel?* What did I feel when the dance craving began, before the anger? I went back over it, and remembered feeling helpless, starved, like a child deprived by an adult.

Step 4. *What does this remind me of?* Before I was married I felt that way sometimes with boy friends; dying to dance, afraid to ask, frustrated and angry. What else did it remind me of? Dancing has special meanings for me. The old Fred Astaire-Ginger Rogers movies colored my daydreams as a girl. I would meet my true love at a dance, we would float in each other's arms and know we were meant for each other . . . Cinderella at the ball.

Suddenly I recalled my father's account of falling in love with my mother while dancing. What else did this remind me of? Dixieland jazz is like ragtime. I lived with my unmarried aunts after my parents separated when I was five. They lived such glamorous, grownup lives; dates and dancing. They danced to ragtime in those days! But still no hidden feeling. I went back again to

Step 3. *What else did I feel?* Frustrated because Bernie did not ask me to dance. Why couldn't I ask him to dance? Afraid of rejection. So what? What if he said he was too tired, or not in the mood? What would happen? How would I feel? Ashamed. *Shame.* That was the hidden feeling. I was ashamed of this craving to dance. The shame was so painful that I began to cry. But it only lasted about a minute and then it was all over. (The anger against Bernie had disappeared as soon as the shame took over.) I felt relieved and refreshed, ready for the next step.

Step 5. *Look for the pattern.* Now I could see my pattern. Whenever I felt that craving to dance I was secretly ashamed of it. That was why I could not tell Bernie. This silence was self-defeating in two ways. a) I forced him to deprive me. b) Then I reacted to this deprivation as if he were deliberately punishing me for my shameful desire. This made the hidden shame more intense. Why was I ashamed of dancing? What did dancing symbolize for me? I did not know. I am not my own psychiatrist. I do not have to understand myself; all I can do is peel away one layer of the onion (which is me) at a time and feel what lies underneath. I hoped some day I might peel away another, deeper layer and learn more. (Later, I did.) Meanwhile, I could see my pattern. I was predictable to myself. I would probably get that craving again, be tempted to feel shame and cover up with anger again.

It is rarely necessary or wise to share your hidden feeling with the person directly involved, but I needed Bernie's help. I did not want him to be a good listener, to help me with self therapy in this case, so I waited another day to be sure the whole thing had cooled off. Then I gave him a brief outline: how I had been dying to dance

11

but was afraid to ask him, how I had been irrationally angry (now that the anger was gone, it was safe to tell him), how I was afraid I might repeat the whole thing again. Bernie was dumbfounded. How could I be in such a turmoil without giving him a clue? Why should I be ashamed of wanting to dance? He was no mind reader; I would have to tell him how I felt. Sure, he might be tired, not feel like dancing, but that didn't mean rejection or punishment or anything like that.

Some months later we were at a dinner dance and the band played Dixieland. Along came that familiar, frantic, starved feeling. This time I plucked up courage after a minute and casually (!) suggested dancing. But Bernie had just put away an enormous meal and needed time for digestion before cavorting to Dixieland. For a minute this stirred up all the old frustration and rage. Then I remembered the hidden shame and the picture changed; he was not punishing me. He had every intention of dancing later. The evening was still young. The anger melted away and I could relax and wait patiently for Bernie to be ready as he was in a little while.

That was the last time I had trouble with my dancing urge. Little by little after that I began to change. For one thing, I revived an early interest in modern interpretive dancing (see my chapter, "How to Free Your Natural Creativity") and discovered I could enjoy Dixieland all by myself. After I stopped forcing Bernie to deprive me, by my silence, I became less dependent on him for this pleasure. Lately I notice I have outgrown that old compulsion. I still enjoy dancing, but the childish craving has disappeared.

COMMUNICATION BETWEEN PARENT AND CHILD

PART I. THE PARENT'S MESSAGE

WE ARE a generation of anxiety-and-guilt-ridden parents. Thanks to the child guidance experts, we know now that children need love, warmth, acceptance and emotional security. But no one tells us how to become the kind of parent who can give all these things. How do you turn on warmth and acceptance like a hot-water faucet when you are feeling cold and rejecting? Authoritarianism is out of date. We are advised to be permissive—but not too permissive! Set limits— but don't be too rigid! No psychology book will tell us when to be permissive and when to use discipline; there are no blue prints for human relations.

Here is one general guide-line that helps. Be permissive to your child's *feelings* even when you must set limits to his *actions*. Is he jealous of the new baby? Teach him to hit a rubber doll and call it baby. Does he stamp his little foot and tell you he hates you, you mean Mommy, when you drag him in out of the rain (he was having such fun in the puddles)? Let him know that's OK. Little boys can be angry with the people they love. You are not frightened or angered by his rage.

If you can accept his feelings, he will learn to accept them too. He must learn, if he is to become a stable adult, that he is a member of the human family, capable of all kinds of human feelings: fear, jealousy, hate.

You must set limits to his actions where his welfare and the rights of others are involved, but he has a right to feel angry. The message parents need to communicate is: it is alright to feel any emotion at all, but you cannot do things which are dangerous to yourself or others.

This is all very well in theory. The trouble is we cannot accept our children's feelings unless we can accept our own. You cannot be permissive to anyone else when you are cruel to yourself.

I had a student whose pre-school child had terrible temper tantrums. The mother tried to help him overcome them. She avoided unnecessary frustrations, supplied him with materials recommended for "channeling aggression" finger-paints, water-play, mud-pies, hammer-and-peg toys, even a punching-bag), all in vain. Finally she used self therapy and discovered she was really afraid of anger in any form. She never dared feel it herself. She began to realize that every time her little boy had a temper tantrum she was frightened. She guessed that she was communicating her fear to him.

A child suffering a temper tantrum is really suffering. (I do not mean the kind of act some children deliberately put on to assert themselves.) It is a terrifying experience, so powerful that it overwhelms him. He has no control over himself. He is helpless and scared, something like a mentally ill person having a psychotic attack. He needs comfort and reassurance that this will pass, that he will feel better soon. (Read Fritz Redl's books, *Children Who Hate* and *Controls from Within.*) This mother could not give the support her child needed. She could only add her own fear to his. Shortly after she recognized and *felt* her hidden fear of anger, the child's temper tantrums began to taper off, and finally stopped altogether.

A father told me this story. His wife was having trouble toilet-training their two-year-old. This little girl was unusually bright; she talked at an early age and seemed to understand everything said to her. She no longer wet herself, but was still soiling and family life had deteriorated to a battle of wills between mother and child. Bribes, threats, spankings were useless. Spankings became more violent as the mother's despair and rage increased.

One day when the mother was out, the father had charge of his little girl. During the afternoon he put her on her little "toidy" seat, and to his surprise and delight she proceeded to have a bowel movement. He was just about to praise her for this socially-approved accomplishment when the little creature looked up at him piteously and said, "Daddy, don't hit me!"

She had never understood what all the excitement was about. She thought she was being punished for performing a natural function (Shame on you! That's dirty!). How could an intelligent child make such a tragic mistake? Harry Stack Sullivan said children learn to obey simply to maintain our love and approval, not out of fear. A loved child is not emotionally damaged by an occasional spanking (although it teaches him nothing except the power of the strong over the weak) as long as it is not too violent. But if the punishment is too painful or the parent's rage is too irrational, the child has a kind of amnesia for the entire experience and *cannot learn*. This mother obviously had hidden feelings about the toilet-training process which trapped her into self-defeating behavior. She failed to communicate a simple message. Her anxiety and violence got in the way.

Children who learn to speak early confuse their parents. They seem to understand us, they seem to be using the language to communicate, but they are really playing with words; words do not always have the same meaning for them as for us. An eighteen-month-old is scolded and slapped for touching fragile brac-a-brac. Later he glances at his mother and then makes a dash for the forbidden object. "Look at that little devil! He's trying to get a rise out of me," his mother says. But he was only looking at her to get the cue (Is this safe or dangerous?) since her explanation about untouchable things merely confused him, and he is driven by a healthy human need to explore. Easier to baby-proof the house for a while. Do we want to teach our children that curiosity (the basis of all learning) is dangerous? "But they must learn they can't have everything they want," parents protest. Life is full of frustrations for any child growing up in a complicated civilization. The fewer frustrations he has in his early years, the less self-control expected from him before he is capable of it, the more self-control and tolerance for frustration he will have in later years. Afraid you will spoil him? The "spoiled" child is one who has been given material things in place of love, whose parents are permissive because of their hidden fear or guilt. Such a child gets the hidden message, the meaning of the gifts, and is not fooled by the pseudo-kindness.

Sometimes a parent sends two conflicting messages. One may be conscious and direct: follow the golden rule, be a good citizen, obey the law, be a credit to your parents. The other message is unconscious and communicated in subtle ways: tone of voice, facial expression, gestures, posture, words spoken without full awareness of their true meaning. This kind of message comes from the parent's hidden feelings and he does not know what it is, or that he is sending it out. Tragically, the hidden message may be more powerful than the conscious one it contradicts; the child, without realizing it, is obliged to *obey the hidden message*. Bribes, threats, punishment cannot stop him from fulfilling his parent's hidden desires. A respectable, law-abiding father, with a hidden yen to be a devil of a fellow, may preach good citizenship, bemoan the family disgrace when his son

15

becomes delinquent, and punish him cruelly, but the boy cannot help living out his father's secret dream. The father gets a hidden pleasure from the son's misdeeds and metes out doubly harsh punishment because of his own hidden guilt. In the same way, a rigid mother with a hidden longing for forbidden fruit may live vicariously in a daughter who obeys the hidden message and becomes promiscuous. Or a parent, for hidden reasons, feels toward a certain child as if he were someone from the parent's past: an alcoholic brother, a prostitute mother, a violent father. The parent constantly expects the child to turn out "just like your uncle" and despite threats and punishment the self-fulfilling prophecy comes true. These are extreme and tragic cases. Here is a milder example of the secret message.

When Ann was in the third grade I had trouble getting her to school on time. Although the school bus stopped in front of our house, she failed to make it several days each week. I woke her early every morning, breakfast was ready on time, her clothes laid out, but somehow she was so absorbed telling herself stories that she often spent half an hour pulling on her socks. Whenever Ann missed the bus I would rant and rave and reduce her to tears. Then I would hate myself. Why braid a little girl's hair so carefully and iron ruffles on her dress if you're going to send her off to school with a tear-stained face? We talked about her lateness one day when we were both feeling cozy and calm after school. "Mommy, I don't mean to be late," she explained earnestly. "It just happens."

I had already "analyzed" her problem: she hated school and preferred not to go at all. "Lateness," I told Bernie rather pedantically, "is Ann's unconscious protest against school." So I tried not to make her cry. Each morning, my eye on the kitchen clock, I called out in dulcet tones, "Only a half hour left, dear . . . twenty minutes (not so dulcet) . . . ten minutes, almost ready dear? (controlling myself with difficulty) . . . FIVE MINUTES (screaming). Then I would roll in there like a whirlwind, stuff her into her clothes, all my pent-up fury spouting forth like a volcano. Sometimes she managed to catch the bus, barefoot, with shoes in hand (crying); if she missed it I drove her to school, raging all the way and she got there in time (crying).

One morning, when I had propelled Ann into the bus at the last minute by sheer will power, I was troubled as usual by her tears. I began to tell Bernie for the umpteenth time how I felt. I had never

16

had much help from this quarter, his attitude being, "What's all the fuss about?"

"She has to learn to get to school on time."

"Why? What difference does it make?"

At which I would splutter indignantly about the duty of parents to prepare their children for the demands of real life, etc. and Bernie would merely shrug maddeningly. Despite his lack of understanding on past occasions, I had to unburden myself on this difficult morning. I began to recite my grievances: how I hated to see her start the day in tears, how frantic and helpless I felt at my inability to cope with this problem. "That child has absolutely no sense of time," I wound up. "She's always been like that. It's torture to go anywhere with her, she dawdles so, we always end up waiting for her. What's the matter with her?"

"I don't understand what your problem is," commented Bernie with infuriating calm. "Are you worried about Ann being late to school, or are you trying to change her character?" I was struck dumb. For the first time I *heard* myself. No, I did not want to change her character. She was a lovable, relaxed little thing; that lack of concern about time was part of her easy-going, placid nature which made her so easy to live with (except that our daily hassle was beginning to bring on certain new signs of tension).

For the first time it occurred to me that I was over-reacting to the whole problem. That was Step 1. *Notice inappropriate reaction.*

Step 2. *Feel the apparent emotion.* Well, I was certainly as angry and frustrated as I needed to be.

Step 3. *What else did I feel?* How do I feel when I'm watching the clock in the kitchen before I know whether or not Ann will miss the bus? Can't keep my eye off that minute hand. Tense, fearful. As the minutes tick by the tension grows as if I'm afraid something terrible will happen. What can happen? What am I afraid of? Nothing so simple as Ann's lateness. Something unknown.

"You know something?" I said suddenly to Bernie. "I think I'm irrational about time, about promptness."

Bernie laughted out loud. "You're telling me?" Then I remembered the arguments about going places together, his protests at being hurried off to sit in front of the curtain long before it was scheduled to go up at amateur performances which are notoriously late in starting. Now, thinking about it, it occurred to me that I was compulsive about time.

17

Step 4. *What does this remind me of?* My father is even more rigid about promptness than I. I used to be amused by his obsession with time; I had never realized I was following in his footsteps. So that anxiety, the fear of lateness bringing on unknown disaster I discovered in Step 3, was the hidden feeling under the anger toward Ann.

Step 5. *Look for the pattern.* I did not know why I was irrational about time, but I knew I could not help myself. Ann's tardiness threatened to make me feel anxiety and I covered it up with anger. For the first time I thought, "Ann is irrational about time too. She can't help herself either." Now the whole picture changed; the problem looked different.

That day I bought a clock for Ann's room. "I've been giving you a hard time about being late to school," I told her. "I guess I get too excited about it. You can tell time yourself, so from now on I'll wake you and get breakfast ready, but the rest is up to you. I won't nag you anymore. If you miss the bus I'll drive you, but I may get you there a few minutes late. I'll cook Daddy's breakfast first. I think one reason I've been so upset is the terrible rush to get back in time for that."

Ann was delighted to hear of the new regime, so glad to get me off her back she was not worrying about being late. The next day she missed the bus, and came into the kitchen to hover over me while I fried Bernie's eggs. "When will you be ready to drive me? When?"

"Right away, honey. Soon as I get Daddy's breakfast on the table."

Ann fidgeted and a querulous tone entered her voice. "I'll be late!" This was the *first time* she had ever expressed concern about being late. Up to then I had done all the worrying for her. Finally we drove up to the school about five minutes after the bell. Ann whimpered, "I'm afraid to go in."

"What does the teacher do to you when you're late?"

"I was never late before." She was *never late before!* I had never allowed my child to be late before. I had never given her the opportunity to grapple with the reality of school demands, to learn from actual experience how to get along with the outside world. Too busy with our own private mother-daughter battle. I, who had read all the child psychology books—talk about not using your intelligence and experience!

18

"Well, she won't eat you. What does she do to the others when they're late?"

"They have to stand up in front of the class and tell why they were late."

Not cruel and inhuman punishment, surely, but to a shy child like Ann it could be torture. I did my best to comfort her. "Oh, honey, I'm sorry." I was sincere: the poor kid was scared stiff. "Maybe you'll do better tomorrow." I kissed her goodby. (One mother who heard this story later complained, "I used your method but it didn't work. She's still late." And when I questioned her I found she had rejoiced when the school punished her child, gloated and said, "I told you so!" instead of comforting her.)

I will not say it was a matter of days or even weeks, but in a few months Ann stopped missing the school bus. Did she change her personality, her attitude about time? Not at all. That was eight years ago. Ann still dawdles in the mornings, rushes around madly the last few minutes and flies to school. But she is not late. How she manages to get there on time is her own problem.

Have I changed? No. I wake Ann up, prepare breakfast and keep my eye *off* the clock. I do not know what time the school bell rings. I dare not find out for fear I would be tempted to nag her again. (As a matter of fact, every few years Ann has a spell of tardiness, and each time I take a good look at myself and discover I am back in the same old rut, "helping" her to get out on time, worrying for her, nagging her.) I am still as compulsive about time as ever. I have not peeled away that layer of the onion yet. Perhaps I never shall; but I can use my intellect to keep that irrational impulse from getting in Ann's way. I can remember to mind my own business.

Nowadays I am more aware of my foolish preoccupation with time. I feel that in some ways I am a prisoner of the clock. Sometimes I catch myself envying Ann's freedom from that jailor. Was I sending her a hidden message in those days: be late as I dare not be? It seemed to me then I was doing my best to get her out on time but somehow she did not respond to my efforts. I think she was obeying my secret wish, my hidden envy of the very trait I punished. How did I communicate that hidden message? Perhaps by my tone of voice, the tension in my body, the expression on my face. We do not notice how we sometimes contradict the words we say while we utter them.

I knew a mother who was frantic because her little girl bit other

19

children. Mrs. Jones apologized profusely to the neighbors whenever this happened, scolded and spanked her daughter, but little Janie kept right on biting. One day, when she had just done her best to bite a hunk out of her best friend's arm in a moment of frustration, I caught a glimpse of the mother's face: a mischievous grin flashed across it for a brief moment and was extinguished, displaced by an angry frown. As I watched her fly to the rescue (just too late, as usual, to protect the little victim) and wallop Janie, I had the distinct impression that Mrs. Jones was completely unaware of that smile. I am sure she never recognized the triumphant child within her who gloried in her daughter's aggression; but Janie, on some deep level, understood. She got the message.

One evening I was playing the piano and singing, when my small daughter Jeanie came running in to ask a question, "Can I go to Susie's party Saturday?"

It's hard to answer a question and sing at the same time, but I managed to sandwich the words in between the lines of the song, "Yes, dear."

"What should I wear, Mommy? The new yellow dress? Huh? What should I wear Mommy?"

"Uh-huh, fine, dear." I was trying not to lose my temper.

"But maybe the old blue one is prettier. What do you think, Mommy?"

I am not sure how long this inquisition went on, but it seemed like an eternity while I nodded and smiled grimly and answered in monosyllables, hoping she would shut up soon and let me sing. Finally I lost control and began to scream at the top of my lungs, "Why can't you let me sing? Every time I try to sing you interfere! What's the matter? Can't you stand to hear me? Go in your room and shut the door. You don't have to listen to me!"

The poor child burst into tears. "I'm sorry, Mommy . . . I like you to sing . . . I didn't know . . . I didn't mean . . ."

I was shaking with rage. "Let's take a walk around the block," I begged Bernie. I could not trust myself to go on for fear I would be too cruel to her. So we walked around the block while I let off steam. "She's been this way ever since she was a baby," I complained. "She hates to hear me sing. The minute I get warmed up she starts needling me. I ought to be able to sing in my own house!" Bernie calmly smoked his pipe and let me rave on. After a while I stole a glance at him. "You think I'm over-reacting?" I ventured timidly.

He removed the pipe from his mouth and said mildly, "She's only a child. She didn't know she was bothering you."

Perhaps he was right. I could not stop being angry; maybe I was making a mountain out of a molehill. That was Step 1. *Recognize an inappropriate reaction.* Step 2. *Feel the apparent emotion.* Well, I was as angry as I needed to be, so I could go on to Step 3. *What else did I feel* when Jeanie began to interrupt my singing? How did I feel just before the anger? Tense, anxious; hoping she would leave me alone so I could keep on singing without spoiling my mood. Step 4. *What did this remind me of?* Other times Jeanie and I had gone through similar scenes.

I wasn't getting anywhere. *What did I seem to be doing?* First I became tense and anxious, but I did not tell her to stop. Why not? I let her go on and on until I was furious; I screamed at her, "You don't want me to sing!" But I knew she was busy with her own thoughts and couldn't care less whether I sang or not. She didn't even hear me singing, probably. What did I seem to be doing? I was acting as if I expected her to stop me from singing, as if she had a right to stop me, as if I shouldn't be singing.

What hidden feelings could I possibly have about singing? *What did this remind me of?* I had peculiar attitudes about singing. Although I was a good strong alto in glee club or choir, my solo voice was fragile, feeble, like a little girl's; the piano drowned it out. Somehow I needed to lean on a group before I could let myself go. What did this remind me of? When I was eleven my father remarried and I acquired a beloved stepmother. I tried hard to win Stella's approval in every possible way. She was a real singer with a sensitive ear and when I went around singing slightly off-key it felt to her like chalk scratching on a blackboard. So one day she sat down at the piano and patiently taught me one song. "See," she pointed out, "the next note goes *up;* you're singing it *down* here." With this visual aid I learned to sing that song perfectly ("God Rest Ye Merry Gentlemen"—it was Christmas). "If I'm around when you feel like singing," she warned me, "sing this song only." And I did. (I grew to hate "God Rest Ye Merry —"). Eventually I took piano lessons, my ear improved, I learned to carry a tune and my repertoire increased.

But this was an old story told many times with amusement, resentment, but no hidden feeling. What else did this remind me of? Stella and I sang duets as I improved, and it was always a strain for her

21

to hush her powerful voice so as not to drown out what she called my "peanut whistle." "Louder," she would demand, but the harder I tried, the tighter my throat grew.

What else did this remind me of? My own mother sang too. I had an early memory of her in a kimono with a kind of feather boa that was fashionable in those days, seated at the piano singing a popular song of the time, "Marquita," and looking the most glamorous person in the world to my adoring eyes.

After my father remarried, I was brought up by my father, aunts, and my stepmother, to be different from my mother. "Just like your mother" was a sword that hung over my head whenever I was naughty. But singing? What was wrong with singing? Had I forbidden myself to sing because Mother sang? Still no hidden feeling.

I tried another tack. What about my early feelings about my mother? When my parents separated I was five. I remembered a dramatic scene with shouting and tears, when they used me as a weapon to hurt one another. "Let the child decide," one of them said. "Go on, choose. You want to live with Mother or Daddy?" I remembered how at first I could not choose; I wanted them both. Then I began to feel sorry for Daddy; she was leaving him; she had never loved him I had felt for a long time. I would love him, poor Daddy. So I chose my father.

How did that little girl feel about trying to be a better wife to her father? Guilt for stepping into her mother's shoes? I did not know, but now, telling the story to Bernie, I suddenly burst out, "How could they do that to me? I was only a little girl!" Only a little girl . . . and then I remembered something I had long outgrown. As an adolescent and young adult I had a peculiar habit I never observed until close friends pointed it out. Whenever I was in a threatening situation, among strangers, I had a tendency to talk in a thin, little "baby" voice (remember Gracie Allen?). This was so unlike my usual, unaffected, straightforward self that it embarrassed my friends. It embarrassed me too when I began to notice it, but I had no control over it. I never recognized what I was doing until it was too late. Finally, after I was married, I outgrew it.

Now, for the first time, I *knew* what that baby voice meant. The child within me was saying, "I'm only a little girl." For a few minutes I was that little girl again: alert to the needs of the adults in power, aware of their moods and expectations, skilled in the craft of acting the role my current foster parent preferred, fearful of being

22

found out. I felt like an adult trapped in a child's body in those days, pretending to be a child. Why? Was I afraid that when I took Mother's place father might expect too much of me? Was I afraid of Mother's vengeance, punishment for displacing her? Was it guilt? I did not know (I am not my own psychotherapist); I only knew that singing was a dangerous activity, reserved for grown-up women. The child within me was afraid to sing out like an adult.

Step 5. *Look for the pattern.* In a few minutes I was back again to my safe, adult self once more, and the anger toward my daughter (the apparent emotion) was gone. As always after feeling a hidden emotion, the whole picture changed. I saw now what this evening's scene was all about. I knew why I over-reacted whenever my singing was interrupted.

When Jeanie first began to talk to me I acted as if I had no right to stop her, as if I were doing something wrong, singing. This permissive attitude encouraged her to continue chatting, and the child within me felt more and more threatened, as if Jeanie was telling me I must not sing. The anxiety grew until I became angry. The anger covered up my feeling that she had a right to stop me from doing this forbidden thing.

I could expect to have this trouble again, but now that I knew my pattern, I could use my intelligence and try to nip it in the bud. My vision was clearer now too, the distortion gone, and I could undo some of the immediate damage. I went right home and apologized to Jeanie for flying off the handle. "I guess I'm sensitive about being interrupted when I sing," I explained.

"But Mommy, I didn't know," she protested. "I didn't mean to bother you. I didn't know you minded." Of course she didn't know. When she first asked about the party I had smiled sweetly and acted as if it was perfectly all right to talk to me while I was singing. I had given her the misleading message: keep on talking; don't let me sing.

Now I said to her, "It was my fault. I should have stopped you right away instead of letting you go on until I had to yell. From now on, whenever I sit down at the piano to sing I'll remind you in advance not to interrupt." And that is how I handled it. For a long time after that, I would announce to the family, "Don't anybody talk to me for a while? I want to sing." Sometimes I forgot to warn them, but I found I could shake my head or murmur, "Shush!" and I never had to go through that disturbing scene again.

About a year later Bernie pointed out something new: I had begun to sing in a full, grown-up womanly voice when I sang alone, just as I had always been able to do in the choir. I had finally stopped talking baby-talk.

COMMUNICATION BETWEEN PARENT AND CHILD

PART II. THE CHILD'S MESSAGE

WE MUST be permissive to our children's feelings while setting limits to their action. The problem is: when to use discipline and when to give in, when to be firm and when to be easy. Is this the moment to be accepting so my child will not be afraid of his feelings? Or should I put my foot down so he will know he cannot get away with this? There are no set rules to follow. Each situation must be handled separately; but this is not as difficult as it sounds. So long as you are not hiding anything from yourself, so long as you can afford to feel your own true emotions, your child's behavior is a non-verbal message you can easily understand. When you are open to your own feelings you are open to his message; you can spontaneously, intuitively, respond to his real need without running to the psychology books for guidance. Is he frightened, helpless, hurt? No expert need tell you this is the time to be accepting, to give him the warm support that will strengthen him. Is he doing something dangerous? Hurting someone? Experimenting to see if he can get a rise out of you? These are the times to set limits so he will know the score.

But what happens when you are hiding something from yourself, not aware of your true feelings, covering up? Now you cannot get your child's message; you misinterpret his behavior, fail to understand his need. You feel inadequate as a parent and the problem seems insoluble. You are firm and harsh when he needs acceptance and comfort, soft and permissive when you should be setting limits.

Suppose your little boy comes home from school, and when you greet him with a loving smile he scowls, growls and stomps off to his room slamming the door in your face. If this has been one of your good days and you are feeling safe and comfortably grown-up, not hiding anything from yourself, you ask yourself, "What's eating him?" You may then recall that he is having trouble with his best friend or a difficult teacher. You recognize that he has had a hard day and you have no difficulty choosing between permissiveness or discipline. This is when he needs comfort and you naturally supply it in the acceptable form (kisses, cookies or tactful silence, depending on his age and personality).

But suppose you do not know what is bothering him? As far as you know his social life is fine, his teacher lovely. In this mood of self-acceptance, hiding nothing from yourself, you react in the same way. You can accept your child's anger and spontaneously respond to his unspoken message without intellectual knowledge about his problem. You do not have to understand him: you are his parent, not his psychiatrist.

But take a day when your self-esteem is low. You have done something you are ashamed of, or someone whose approval matters criticized you harshly. You are feeling inadequate. Your little boy comes home on the warpath and you hit the ceiling. (How dare he be so disrespectful, he doesn't deserve such a good mother, spoiled brat, he'd better march right back here and shut that door without slamming; how about an apology, etc.) You cannot imagine why he is acting this way and surely it is your responsibility to teach him manners, set limits, be firm.

Suppose you know he is having trouble with his best friend. This information does not help you: you cannot accept his feelings. (Mustn't take his childish squabbles out on his mother, what are you —a doormat? Must learn self-control.) Intellectual knowledge about your child is not enough to help you respond appropriately to his message as long as you are hiding something from yourself. While you are afraid to feel your hidden feeling, communication is blocked: you cannot hear what he is really saying.

You are angry now. What hidden emotion may be covered by that anger? Only when you peel away a layer of your own psyche will you know. Different people use anger to hide different feelings. You yourself may use anger to cover different emotions at different times.

One parent may have a hidden picture of herself as she would like to be. Like all hidden feelings, this one is unrealistic: the Absolutely Perfect Parent. Without realizing it, she is always trying to live up to this impossible, fantastically exaggerated image. Whenever something threatens to destroy this picture, she is threatened with anxiety which she instantly covers up with anger. When her child is unhappy it means to her she is not a perfect parent.

Another parent has had a miserable childhood, is living vicariously

26

in her child and trying to get a "second chance." Whenever her child is unhappy she feels cheated (Be happy, damn you!) and angry.

Then there is the parent whose child's action threatens to recall something painful from the past. Perhaps her rejecting father slammed doors like this. Her hidden feeling now is helplessness, as if she were the child and her little boy the parent. She covers this up with anger.

When your self-esteem is low you feel inadequate as a parent, perhaps. Then your child's unhappiness is an accusation, threatening to stir up guilt, so you cover it with anger.

Whenever you can look within and feel the emotion you are hiding, you will be able to hear your child's message and know how to answer it.

This happened to me. One evening when the rattling of pots and pans proclaimed the preparation of supper, my older daughter yelled from her room, "When do we eat? I'm *starved!*" We have been eating at the same hour for years, so the unnecessary question and the frantic tone sounded like, "What's the matter with the service in this lousy hotel?"

Naturally I yelled right back, "Stop nagging, act your age, come in and help if you're in such a hurry," and more of the same. This exchange rapidly deteriorated to a hysterical duet. It was not until the next day that I remembered we had been going through this, off and on, for years, that the poor kid couldn't help herself: the strict schedule laid down by the pediatrician made her cry for her bottle the first few weeks of her life, and here she was, still crying. I understood her problem; I had "analyzed" her unconscious motivation long ago. It had never helped me to handle her then and it did not help me now. I could not stand her nagging and I did not know how to shut her up. This was a clue. If you generally get along well with your child, as I do, and you find yourself stuck with one special problem over and over again, chances are you are hiding something from yourself. Why was I handling this problem so awkwardly? That was Step 1. *Notice an inappropriate reaction.*

Step 2. *Feel the apparent emotion.* I was calm now, trying to solve yesterday's problem, so I visited a friend who has a teen-ager too, and told her my story. In no time at all I was re-living yesterday's anger.

Step 3. *What else did I feel?* Now I could recall that when my daughter first began to yell, just before I became angry, I felt terribly tense: as if she were standing over me with a whip and I had to hurry, hurry! When the anger came it released the tension and I forgot it.

Step 4. *What does this remind me of?* I remembered how she had cried for the bottle. But that intellectual understanding did not help: I was still angry (She's a big girl now; how long must she cry for her bottle?). What else did this remind me of? Food . . . my compulsive eating . . . compulsive about feeding my family. How did I really feel years ago when my baby had to cry for her bottle because the pediatrician said feed her every four hours?

For the first time I tried deliberately to re-live that scene instead of simply intellectualizing about it. In my mind's eye I saw the baby's room, felt myself standing just outside her door so she couldn't see me, my eye on my watch, waiting for permission to feed her. I remembered how she screamed, poor little thing, and how I cried with her: tears of helplessness, frustration, anxiety, and . . . *guilt.* That guilt swept over me now in a wave so painful that I began to sob as if I were back there again. The hidden guilt drowned out all the anger. For fifteen years I had been passing the buck, blaming the pediatrician for starving my baby. Now, belatedly, I dared to feel the guilt myself.

Step 5. *Look for a pattern.* The guilt lasted only a minute, and then I could see my pattern. Not the whole design of my relationship with this child, not my basic attitude toward food, nothing so broad. Simply, the pattern that whenever this youngster screams for food, the old hidden guilt is stirred up and threatens to come out and hurt me. First, I tense up and rush around frantically trying to prove what a good mother I am; then, when the tension becomes unbearable, I escape into anger. Next, I act out this self-defeating, pseudo-anger which encourages her to scream louder. This adds to the hidden guilt which I then cover up with more anger, etc.

Now that I saw my pattern, I was predictable to myself. I could look forward to an opportunity to face this problem again and try to handle it another way. I was not sure yet what I would do next time. Sure enough, about a month or two later I heard the same old complaint, "When do we eat? I'm *starved!*" Once again I began to tense up, but this time, just before the tension eased into anger, I remembered that hidden guilt. I did not *feel* it again; all I did was remember it intellectually. Immediately my tension relaxed and the tone of my child's voice said something different to me. Instead of, "What's the matter with the service in this lousy hotel?" it sounded more like, "Mommy, I'm so miserable. Don't you care?"

Of course I cared. Easily, spontaneously, I answered her need, "Right away, honey. Supper's almost ready." That was all she needed to hear: not another peep out of her!

That was four years ago and I have never had trouble with that particular problem since. Neither of us has changed basically: she still nags once in a while when I am preparing supper; I still tend to tense up as if she were accusing me of starving her. But I can always remember the hidden guilt before I need to cover up with anger. Sometimes I say, "Supper's a little late tonight. Come and have a bite to keep you going." I no longer act in the old, stereotyped, self-defeating pattern. I can hear my daughter's message.

Is that guilt a cover for a deeper hidden feeling? Why did I (with my intense feelings about food) deprive my baby? Why did I (not easily awed by authority) obey the pediatrician blindly? Since I have tried hard to atone for that early deprivation and am in general an adequate mother, is it rational for me to continue to carry that burden of guilt? What are my hidden feelings about food?

I do not know: I am not my own psychoanalyst. I peeled away one layer of the onion; undoubtedly there are many other layers underneath. Perhaps some day I shall peel away another. Meanwhile, I am a little freer to use my intelligence and experience to act more like the mother I want to be, despite my irrational impulses: the mother who responds to her child's message.

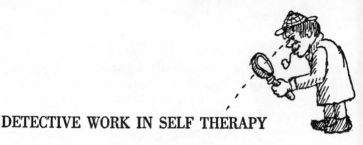

DETECTIVE WORK IN SELF THERAPY

SOMETIMES, BY the time you get around to noticing an inappropriate reaction, it has been going on for such a long time that it is difficult to track down the hidden emotion. This is the time to do some detective work, following up any likely clue.

One morning, as I contemplated dirty dishes and unmade beds, life seemed unusually dreary. Household chores suddenly appeared to be boring drudgery, yet I could not imagine anything else I wanted to do. The day stretched ahead long and dull, nothing to look forward to. I call this a mild depression. The old, recurring deep depression was a thing of the past (see the chapter, "Suffering Can Be Therapeutic"). Mild depression for me is a general distaste for the mechanics of living plus a pervasive boredom. It always means I am hiding something from myself, something I am afraid to feel. That was Step 1. *Notice inappropriate reaction.*

Step 2. *Feel apparent emotion.* Some people are ashamed of depression and try to drown it out with frantic activity or talk themselves out of it ("I'm so lucky; I have everything I need. What right have I to be depressed?") or bully themselves out of it ("Come on now, stop being so sorry for yourself and snap out of it!") It does not help to be angry with yourself for being depressed. Sometimes, of course, you have to escape into some cheering activity (shopping, movies) to give yourself a breather; but if you are feeling strong enough, use the depression for self therapy: let yourself feel it.

Step 3. *What else did I feel?* I could not answer this, because I did not remember when the depression began or what started it, and so I began to do some detective work. How long have I had this symptom? Did I feel this way when I woke up today? That's right, I was too busy cooking breakfast to pay attention but now that I thought back I realized I had felt blue all morning. How about last night? Hmn . . . yes, I guess I was pretty glum at bedtime too. Earlier yesterday? Well, I wasn't very good company at supper, and preparing that meal wasn't much fun either. Yesterday afternoon and morning? I could not remember very clearly, except that I remembered feeling fine yesterday morning. So sometimes between morning and evening yesterday, something happened to set off this depression. What did I do yesterday? Attended a neighborhood tea party; very informal and merry; had a nice time. Did anything unusual happen there? Anything that might have threatened to make me feel some painful emotion?

At first I could not think of anything relevant; then I remembered one young woman, famous for her caustic wit. We had been kidding around and she shrilled in her humorous way, "Oh, Muriel, you always talk so much! Nobody can get a word in edgewise." How did I feel then? Amused. I knew she liked me and she was a great kidder, so I took it in my stride. What else did I feel? Anxious to let her and the others know I was not hurt, that I was a good sport.

Step 4. *What does this remind me of?* Good sport. Bernie has often accused me of being a compulsive good sport. (Actually, his words were "good-natured slob"). Was it possible that underneath I was hurt by what she said? Oh no, I couldn't be so childish. We all knew this was just her style; she always horsed around like that. If I were an outsider looking on, *what would it look as if I were doing?* What emotion might I be hiding? Anger?

And the funny thing is, the moment I asked myself that question, as soon as I thought the word "anger," anger came gushing out. I was furious. How dared she say such an outrageous thing! She and her phony sophistication, that cat! And more of the same. I was hopping mad for about two whole minutes and then it was all over. I felt fine: the apparent feeling, the depression, was gone. I proceeded to wash dishes and make beds with gusto and I had a lovely day.

Step 5. *Look for the pattern.* Why am I a compulsive good sport? I did not find out until years later, exploring a different problem, But I did notice something else after I felt that hidden anger.

That same witty neighbor once criticized my housekeeping and it did not bother me: I am not house proud. Tell me I am not beautiful and I can take it in my stride: I am used to my face. Tell me I am stupid and I'll probably laugh: I know darn well I'm not stupid. I have no hidden feelings in these areas. But talking too much has some painful meaning for me. Shame? Guilt? I do not know yet: I am still working on it through self therapy whenever the occasion arises.

31

That day I recognized my pattern for the first time. I have hidden feelings about talking, about communicating, which make me so sensitive to any criticism that I cover it up with depression. This experience paved the way for further exploration and years later I peeled away another layer, found out more about the hidden meaning of words for me, and managed to get over a writing block.

WRITING AS A PATH TO THE HIDDEN FEELING

SO FAR I have described two paths to the hidden feeling: a) talking to a good listener and b) thinking it through alone. Now I want to discuss a third way, the writing technique.

There are several points to keep in mind if you are planning to use this approach. You must be *in the midst of an emotional experience.* If you sit down to write about a problem in cold blood you may end up with the story of your life, but that is not self therapy. The purpose of self therapy is to feel the emotion you are hiding *right now,* not merely theorize about your past. You must start with an apparent emotion. Write while this cover feeling is hot off the griddle: do not wait till it cools off.

Forget about punctuation, spelling, legibility, grammar: no one will read this but you. You are talking to yourself.

Try to write at a steady pace, without stopping. Put all your thoughts on paper. If the ideas are coming slowly, stall for time: write out the questions as well as the answers, just to keep writing. The constant, steady flow of words seems to have a hypnotic effect that loosens up hidden feelings.

Write with a soft pencil; make it easy for yourself. Do not use a typewriter even if you hate to write and think a typewriter is easier. It does not work. Perhaps it is too mechanically perfect. The pencil seems to become an extension of your body: as your emotion grows more intense your writing becomes larger and wilder and less legible.

You need privacy. If necessary, keep pencil and paper in the bathroom and lock yourself in there to write while the apparent emotion is still intense. If you cannot possibly get off by yourself to write in the midst of an emotional experience, try to revive it as soon afterward as possible. Talk about it to a good listener until you can feel the apparent emotion again; then get off by yourself and write.

Writing is the quickest way I know to find a hidden feeling. The whole process should not take more than ten to twenty minutes. If you find yourself writing for hours, you are doing something else, perhaps creative writing, but that is not what I mean by self therapy.

What kinds of apparent feelings should lead you to use the writing technique? a) An inappropriate reaction: an emotion which you suspect is a cover for something hidden. b) Any emotion so painful you can hardly bear it. Writing will help you get rid of some of it. c) A feeling that tempts you to act out, when your intellect says do nothing. Writing will help channel it.

Write the question, *What am I feeling?* Begin by describing your apparent emotion. Angry with your wife? Write all the nasty things you would never say aloud. Write anything that will help you feel that apparent emotion more intensely.

Suppose you do not know what your apparent emotion is. You feel only physical discomfort: tense, shaky, you have palpitations, you are short of breath; something is bothering you but you do not know what it is. *Describe your physical symptoms.* Clenching your jaw or the muscles in your back? Write about it.

What happened? What started this feeling? Review the incident that set you off.

What might have been bothering me? What might I have been afraid to feel?

What does this remind me of?

All these questions are attempts to get a rise out of you. Your intellect is trying to get some emotional response. Remember, you are not at this moment trying to understand yourself intellectually. The purpose of writing is to feel a hidden emotion. Try different answers to your questions until one brings on an emotional reaction. Suppose you think of an answer that seems logical, a clever explanation for your apparent feeling and your self-defeating behavior; but it is merely an idea without emotion. Drop it: go on to another thought. Do not let yourself be side-tracked by clever intellectualizing. Put those bright ideas away for another time. They may be correct, but if you are not ready to feel them now, they are not useful to you at this moment. Avoid the temptation to theorize at length about your unconscious motivation: this is just another way of covering up the hidden emotion, a device to avoid feeling. Go back and ask yourself once again, What *else* does this remind me of?

Keep trying new ideas. Within ten to twenty minutes you will probably hit one thought that either brings forth an intense hidden emotion or starts a mild new emotion. In the latter case, let your mind wander freely along these new lines: write anything that occurs to

34

you relevant to the new idea, no matter how far-out. This should bring you to an intense hidden emotion.

How do you know when you have peeled away a layer and discovered the hidden feeling? It feels at least as intense as the apparent emotion with which you began, and completely displaces it: you remember the apparent emotion but you no longer feel it.

The hidden feeling may be painful, but it should not last more than a minute or two. It is hard to hold on to that hidden feeling and the slightest distraction will dispel it. In the chapter, "Thinking Out Loud," I mentioned Karen Horney's statement, in her book, *Self Analysis,* that you have a built-in, self-protective mechanism that keeps you from uncovering an emotion you are not yet strong enough to feel without undue anxiety. As far as I know this is true, yet I feel I must warn students: if your hidden emotion, when you let it out, stays with you, against your will, longer than a few minutes; if it overwhelms you and you cannot easily throw it off; then self therapy is not for you. Do not use it without professional help. (No student has ever reported such a problem in the nine years I have been teaching self therapy.)

Now that you have felt your hidden feeling you are ready to look for a pattern, just as in the thinking and talking methods.

When you are finished, destroy the paper. Do not save it (unless you are doing this with professional help and your therapist wants to read it). There are two reasons for this: a) Today your self-esteem was strong; you were brave enough to feel this hidden emotion. You may forget it after a while. Then a day comes when you are feeling low: someone was unkind to you, or you did something you are ashamed of. You are cleaning out a drawer and come across this scrap of paper which reveals a hidden emotion you have forgotten and which you *cannot afford to feel* today. You read it and are forced to feel something too painful. This is like having a lay person interpret for you, tell you what you are hiding from yourself before you are ready to find it for yourself, force you to feel. You may become very anxious or depressed.

b) Another reason to discard what you have written. Suppose you forget this hidden feeling. That means you are not ready to remember it; you will have to find it again some day with self therapy, following up another clue, exploring another inappropriate reaction. Each time you re-discover this hidden feeling you are closer to the goal: some day you will spontaneously remember it and discard the cover

35

feeling permanently. There is no short cut. Suppose, after forgetting your hidden feeling, you find your paper and read all about it. That stops you from re-discovering it. You will be *thinking about* your emotions, instead of *feeling* them. No one ever got better that way. It is the kind of game played by people who study psychology in order to intellectualize about themselves as just one more "interesting" case history. They "understand" all about their unconscious motivation, but keep on using the old, self-defeating patterns of behavior. They use all the psychiatric jargon and can glibly discuss their unresolved Oedipus complexes but their lives are not changing. Self therapy means learning to feel. Do not use the writing technique as a gimmick to avoid feeling.

Here are two examples of the writing technique.

I

One day I was driving along a main thoroughfare when two teen-age boys on bikes suddenly darted out from a side street in front of me. They were busy yelling to one another, riding two abreast, and I was not sure they noticed my car close behind them, so I tooted my horn. They looked at me over their shoulders and shouted derisively, "Ah, shut up!"

For an instant rage swept over me in a hot wave. Then I swallowed it down and continued calmly on my way. By the time I reached my destination ten minutes later, I had forgotten all about it. But my teeth ached: that familiar tension which warns me of an oncoming headache. I asked myself, "What's bothering me? What am I afraid to feel?" I did not know. Then, "What happened?" I remembered the boys on bikes and the fact that I had been briefly angry, but the anger was gone; I just felt this terrible tension. I pulled out a small notebook I carry in my purse for just such occasions, and began to scribble, hoping I could get rid of the ache in my teeth in time to avoid a headache (which usually lasts three days). This is what I wrote:

"Teeth ache. Boys turned corner seemed oblivious of car. Blew horn to warn them, fearful for their safety. Fear of my hostility? [Apparently no emotional response to this question, as I dropped it.] Ah, shut up! Felt helpless furious wished I could speak to their parents. Get them in trouble. Go back and run them over. [These words astounded me.] Teach them to appreciate warning.

I give. Would like to make them suffer. Feel self righteous. God-like. Also foolish, helpless. Ashamed of receiving ingratitude & hostility? Biting back bitter words? [To explain aching teeth.] Much angrier at helpless bicyclists & pedestrian children than adult drivers. [A brand new thought.] Identifying with helpless children who don't know they're helpless? As I was?"

Hate ingrates. Feel generous. Hate those who cannot use what At this point I felt a pang of grief and my teeth stopped aching; the apparent feeling, anger, was gone. So I stopped writing.

What was that all about? The moment I wrote, "Identifying with helpless children who don't know they're helpless? As I was?" the memory of two terrible years with a sadistic foster mother flashed through my mind. A few years earlier, talking it out in self therapy, exploring a different apparent feeling, I had dared to feel belatedly the anguish my seven to nine-year-old self had stoically swallowed down: painful experiences I had avoided thinking about all my life. At that time, in the presence of a good listener, I had finally broken down and cried like a helpless child. Now, writing about my experience with these boys it was enough to remember that earlier self therapy session and feel momentary sadness. That was all I needed to get rid of the ache in my teeth and avoid the headache. A psychologist might explain that my childhood rage toward my foster mother turned inward, and that now I was projecting it outward toward those boys. I certainly did not think of anything like that at the time. I was not looking for an explanation of my reactions: I am not my own psychoanalyst. All I needed to do was feel my hidden emotion.

II

Another example. One day I sat down to write the chapter in this book entitled, "How to Free Your Natural Creativity." I wrote the chapter heading at the top of the page. Then I stopped writing and began to think. Now this is not my general writing pattern. Usually my only problem is forcing myself to sit down and pick up the pencil. (I keep telling myself to wash the kitchen floor first, iron some shirts, anything to avoid writing. But once I get started the words flow as fast as I can get them down, especially with this book since I have been teaching this stuff for nine years; the ideas are at my fingertips.

But this time I could not get started. I got up and began to rummage around in the bookcase. I leafed through books I know by heart, tracking down resource material, other people's theories about creativity, to back up my own ideas. This was absurd since I have all that material in my head. I've been lecturing for years without notes. The more I puttered around the more difficult it was to get started writing. I wasted about an hour reading and thinking and playing with words, before it occurred to me that I *could not start writing*. Furthermore, I noticed my throat felt sore. Was I coming down with something, or was this tension? I decided, if I couldn't write my chapter, I would write for self therapy and find out what was going on. So I used that very same page, with the chapter title on top, "How to Free Your Natural Creativity." I wrote:

"Throat hurts. Why? Blocking on creativity. What am I afraid of? Suddenly have to check references. Don't trust myself? Why? What happened? I discovered this method [experiments with creativity described in that chapter] & am using others' theories to explain it. What's wrong with that? Do I feel I am not original because I need their explanation? Creativity means originality. Am I afraid to trust my originality? Fearful that I am not creative? [So far, no emotion.] What does creative mean? [Trying a new angle.] To create a child. To be capable of childbearing. Tears now. Afraid to lose my uterus. [Doctor had warned I might need surgery.] Afraid of hysterectomy. Won't be creative any more. Will I be a changed person? Not a creative person any more. Yes."

I was really feeling sorrow now so I stopped writing. The pain in my throat was gone.

Strangely enough, a few weeks earlier, after a medical check-up, I had been told I might need an operation because of a fibroid tumor. At that time I could not feel any emotion. My muscles were tense all day, I was mildly depressed in the evening, but I could not figure out what was bothering me. I did not know what I felt. I was so near menopause, the doctor said, that I probably would not need surgery: such tumors tend to dry up at that time of life. Hysterectomy is a common operation (some of my best friends, etc.) and I was not afraid of surgery.

It was not until now, using self therapy to explore my writing block, that I got a glimpse of my hidden feelings about that operation. I felt extreme sorrow for a few seconds and then I felt fine: it was all over. I was able to dash off that chapter on creativity in record time, without any more trouble.

SNEAKING UP ON THE HIDDEN FEELING

SO FAR, I have described three paths to the hidden emotion: a) talking, b) thinking and c) writing. Now I want to show you a more devious way: a back door to the hidden feeling.

Any aesthetic experience, any form of passive recreation that moves you, is material for this fourth approach to self therapy. A play, opera, ballet, concert, scenic beauty, literature: anything that makes you *feel*. Weeping in the midst of a sad movie? Never mind that everybody else seems to be doing so too: each one is crying for his own personal reasons. Each one brings to the movie his own background, his own history. Each thinks he is suffering in sympathy with the hero and heroine, but something in his own past is re-kindled by this story, and that something may have nothing directly to do with the ill-starred lovers on the screen.

Here is a marvelous opportunity to feel some long-hidden emotion; much easier than with other self-therapy methods. With the talking, thinking and writing techniques you are trying to solve some real-life problem, exploring some inappropriate reaction. Your self-esteem is already a little wobbly with the awareness of some self-defeating behavior, some inappropriate reaction. You may be trying to find a hidden emotion, but you know it will be painful and the fear of such pain slows up the whole process of self therapy. It takes courage to peel away a layer and feel what lies underneath.

But feeling a painful emotion at a movie is very different. Here you are not involved with your own real life: no shame or guilt or fear to hamper you. Ostensibly, this sad story unfolding before you has nothing to do with you: you feel safe. You are not afraid of what you will discover if you peel away a layer, so it is easier than usual to do so. You are sneaking up on the hidden feeling.

Another thing: the process of self therapy usually requires you to stop thinking like a sophisticated adult for a few minutes and revert to an earlier, childlike mental process. This is especially true when you have to re-live a very early experience. It is hard to let go, to give up the control, the intellectual approach that makes you feel grown-up and safe. This is what makes self therapy (any psycho-therapy) so difficult. When you are lost in a story, a symphony, a movie, you have already taken that important step. Your adult intel-lectual processes are no longer in complete control: you are feeling on an earlier, more primitive and childlike level. (See the chapter on creativity.) This makes it easier to go further and feel a hidden emotion.

Steps for a back door to the hidden feeling: You first notice your-self feeling some strong emotion, maybe grief or anger during a movie, play, or concert. Concentrate on that emotion; let yourself feel it as intensely as possible. Then, while you are still feeling it, ask yourself, "What does this remind me of? What am I really upset about?" You may suddenly recall an event, a relationship, a problem from your past. Try now to relive that period and feel the emotion that once was appropriate for that long-ago time. This method can bring you back to very early experiences. You may be able to feel belatedly something you have often thought about but have been unable to feel with other techniques.

Students sometimes ask, "How can you keep your mind on an emotion and explore it while the movie is in progress? Doesn't the action on the screen, the story, distract you from self therapy?" No, not really. Just concentrate on your immediate feeling. If necessary, close your eyes. The whole process is so rapid that you do not miss much of the picture. I have never had any difficulty with this, al-though I guess you could retreat to the washroom to get away from distractions, if you had to.

Another popular question, "Why should I use self therapy every time I cry at a movie? Is it always a neurotic symptom?" No, of course not. It is human and normal to sympathize with another's trouble. This aspect of self therapy is not designed to explore self-defeating, inappropriate behavior. I am merely saying that you are able to weep for someone else because you have something in your own experience that makes his problem meaningful to you. So this is a rare chance to reach a hidden feeling through the back door, to take it by surprise. Why waste it? We do foolish things every day which we cannot afford to notice. How often we pass the buck, blame Fate or the other fellow for our misfortunes. How many times we miss the cue that here is an inappropriate reaction, good material for self therapy. Here, watching a movie, is a chance to make up for those other times when we are not strong enough to use self therapy

41

in connection with our real life problems. The more hidden feelings you feel, the healthier you can become; so use all the material that comes your way.

What if you are so carried away by the story that it does not occur to you to use it for self therapy? Can you use it later, after you get home? Yes, if you are still feeling that emotion by the time it occurs to you to use it; or if you can revive it in some way: thinking about the movie or talking about it. It is a waste of time, however, to "analyze" your feeling after it has cooled off, in cold blood. Your purely intellectual guess will probably be wrong, but even if it is right it cannot help you because you are not feeling the hidden feeling.

I

I went to see the Bolshoi Ballet do "Swan Lake." The magnificent costumes, together with the romantic music and the dancers' technical skill, combined to form a fairyland where my adult skepticism was suspended and I sat open-mouthed and trusting as a child. As the familiar, tragic fairytale unfolded, I sank deeper and deeper into this childlike trance, lost in that fantasy world on the stage. Then came the scene where the Prince realizes in horror that he has been deceived by the wicked Sorcerer: has mistaken the false Black Swan for his own true love, the White Swan. We hear her haunting motif and see the White Swan beckon to him in a vision. He realizes he is condemned to lose her forever; he reaches out for her in an agony of longing and frustration as she fades from view and the curtain falls.

I was terribly shaken and felt like crying. Lights went on, people started strolling out for intermission cigarettes, and I realized how absurd it was for an adult to cry about a fairytale. But I have learned not to waste such opportunities, so I sat still during intermission, my eyes welling up with tears, and let myself feel the dreadful pathos of one who loses his beloved. When the feeling was intense, I asked, "What does this remind me of? Whom did *I* lose?" And the answer was there waiting for me: my mother! I was five when my father took me away from her. In those early years I could not fully take in my loss, could not cry about it, could not believe it was a permanent arrangement. I was too busy with the mechanics of living: adjusting to ensuing foster parents, new schools, new friends. Perhaps a small child cannot afford to feel the depth of tragedy: he has not developed enough emotional strength to face the whole truth. Several adults have told me they could not cry at the funeral of beloved parents in childhood; could not take in the reality of their loss.

So there I was, forty years later, finally letting the child within me cry. As often happens in self therapy, I had a chance to feel belatedly something I should have felt long ago. Sitting there in the theatre, I felt like a small child crying pitifully for her mother. I had to muffle my sobs in a handkerchief (the adult in me was still functioning and did not want to make a fool of herself publicly). The hidden feeling lasted about two minutes and then I was refreshed as I usually am after self therapy, free to enjoy the rest of the show.

II

I went to see the Italian movie "Two Women." The pathos of a mother in a war-torn world trying vainly to protect her beloved daughter broke my heart. I had not yet evolved the back door technique so I did not stop to ask myself, "What does this remind me of?" But I could not get it out of my mind. All the way home, and then later that evening I kept thinking about it, kept feeling that terrible sense of tragic grief.

After several hours of this obsessive thinking it occurred to me this movie might have hidden meanings for me. While I was in the midst of this feeling, crying, identifying with that mother in her fear and grief, I asked myself, "What does this remind me of? What has this got to do with me?" Immediately the answer came, "Some day I will live through a terrible catastrophe: Bernie dead, life not worth living, obliged to go on because my children need me, but helpless to protect them." This fear came out of hiding as if it had been waiting there for years and I wept in terror for my own dreaded future. After a minute it was all over: I felt relaxed and was able to stop my obsessive thinking about the movie. The hidden emotion went back under for the time being, after its brief airing.

A few years later I saw another Italian film, "The Five Days of Naples." Here too was a mother trying to find protection for her children in a war-torn country. Once again I was overwrought with grief. I asked myself, "What does this remind me of?" but all I could do was remember the hidden feeling (fear of the future) that I discovered from the other movie. It was no help this time. I knew the time had come to peel away another layer, so that evening I talked about the movie to Bernie and got all worked up again. What did it remind me of? Identifying with the children because I lost my own mother at five? No new feeling came, so I went on to another angle, closing my eyes and reliving the most pitiful scenes in the picture. My face grew swollen, my eyes sore, and I am sure poor Bernie was sick of the whole thing, but I kept on stubbornly: What does this remind me of?

At last the answer came: "I was that mother." For the first time I began to talk about the year my first child was born. Bernie was a soldier overseas; the responsibility of parenthood terrified me; none of my friends had babies yet and I had no mother around to advise me. All that year I wrote cheerful letters to Bernie, hiding from him and *from myself* the depths of my inadequacy, the fear that I might fail somehow to protect this precious, fragile morsel of life with which he had entrusted me. Facing the truth at last, I went back and lived through the anxiety of that first year. In a few minutes I was finished and could forget about the movie and my own past difficulties. The first movie, "Two Women," had peeled away one layer, fear of the future. The second movie gave me a chance to go deeper and relive the past fear which lay underneath it.

The memory of this hidden feeling has helped me in my relationship with this first child of mine. Sometimes when I am very angry with her, I can recognize that the anger is inappropriate, self-defeating; then I use self therapy and feel once again the old anxiety and helplessness (I am not the Absolutely Perfect Mother: I do not know all the answers), and I can discard that pseudo-anger and handle the situation more intelligently.

Remember, when you use the back door to the hidden feeling, you may not be able to figure out your pattern right away; you may not know just how to use this new information about the child within you. But each time you peel away a layer you have something new to work with. Use your self-knowledge at the first opportunity.

There are some covers, neurotic symptoms, I never explored with self therapy, but which have disappeared during these past seventeen years. I have been trying to feel as many hidden feelings as possible all this time and evidently I have discarded old defenses (covers, inappropriate reactions) which are no longer necessary, without knowing exactly when or how.

When using the "back door" to the hidden emotion, the same basic rule holds true as in any of these self therapy techniques: you must feel the apparent emotion. If you try to figure out why you cried at yesterday's movie without re-living that surface feeling, you will probably make some interesting guesses based on your intellectual knowledge of yourself but chances are you will not discover what you were afraid to feel yesterday. The movie, "David and Lisa," has a heartbreaking scene in an art gallery. The young schizophrenic girl climbs into the lap of a large statue of a seated woman; she snuggles down into blissful sleep, as in the arms of a mother. When forcibly removed and dragged away she weeps and clings pitifully to the statue. I felt intense sorrow at this point. I asked myself what it meant to me personally, what it reminded me of. This poor child seeking love from a marble statue must have been terribly deprived of mother love in her early life. Her tragic need reminded me of the inadequate mother I was when my first child was very small. Not that I was unloving, but so filled with anxiety and insecurity that my love could not be as reassuring as it should have been. My hidden feeling was guilt, as if the girl on the screen was my own little daughter looking for love from a statue, and I was heartbroken.

Later I discussed this same movie with a student to whom that same scene was very moving. He too had used self therapy to discover his hidden feeling. But when he asked himself what this reminded him of, he suddenly felt that he himself was the child desperate for a mother's love. Interestingly enough, his mother was an over-possessive one, and I lost my mother when I was five. If I had been trying, in cold blood, to understand, intellectually, what that scene meant to me I should have guessed I was identifying with the deprived child.

I went to see "Il Trovatore." In this opera is a scene where the old gypsy tells how she attempted vengeance on the Duke who had killed her mother, by throwing his infant son into the fire, how she discovered her gruesome mistake: she had destroyed her own baby. The music and acting combined with the story to send cold chills down my spine; I froze in horror. Then I asked myself, "What does this remind me of?" and once again I had to suffer the old, hidden guilt, regret the stupid mistakes I had made as a young mother. For a horrible moment I *was* that old witch, sobbing out her terrible loss and remorse. This was a hidden feeling that would never have occurred to me if I had waited until I was cool and calm to think about it. On the contrary, I would probably have guessed that the ugly old woman reminded me of the cruel foster-mother who made my life Hell from the ages of seven to nine. I used to tell myself then she was really a witch, not human.

45

I have just illustrated how a movie and an opera, two different kinds of experiences, led me to feel the same hidden emotion: guilt about my role as parent. On the other hand, the same experience which stirs up the identical apparent emotion may, at different times in our lives, reveal different hidden emotions. Years ago, when I was still mourning my stepmother's death, I went to the opera with my father. We saw "Rigoletto," the tragic tale of the court jester who was procurer for his master, the Duke, and who eventually was trapped by his own clever intrigue. In the final heartrending scene Rigoletto discovers that he has inadvertantly caused the death of his beloved daughter, and I wept with him, this poor father suffering loss and frustration and guilt. But when I asked myself what I was *really* crying about, what this reminded me of, something else came out. I was identifying, not with the father, but with the dying daughter and my hidden feeling was the hope that my father would care as much as Rigoletto, that he loved me that much.

Many years later, when I was a parent myself, I saw another performance of "Rigoletto" and was moved once again by that final scene. Once again my apparent feeling was pity for the father's suffering; but when I peeled away a layer I found myself identifying with him in a special way. I was feeling guilt for my own mistakes and inadequacies as a parent. In the intervening years between the first and the second performance I had done a great deal of hard work in self therapy; I had dared to feel many of my hidden feelings about my father. Evidently I was ready now to grow up and feel like a parent.

Several years after that I saw "Rigoletto" once more. As usual I was terribly upset by that pitiful father-daughter scene. As usual it felt like nothing more than pity for that man on the stage. This time, when I asked myself, "What does this remind me of?" the answer was different. I thought what a devoted father Bernie is and how he would suffer if something happened to his daughter. For years I had been exploring my own feelings and examining my own failures; now at last I was ready to feel true concern for someone else, my husband.

COMMUNICATION IN MARRIAGE

EACH OF us has some forbidden feelings he hides from himself: everyone is irrational once in a while. This is what makes human relationships so complicated, especially where people are emotionally dependent on one another, as in marriage. When the person you love suddenly seems irrational, simply will not listen to reason, life can be painful. Why is he irrational? Because something in this situation threatens to make him feel an old, forbidden emotion. He is so busy concentrating on the pseudo-emotion he needs for a cover, that he cannot see things clearly. The fake feeling, as usual, is inappropriate to the present situation, so he appears irrational.

As long as you yourself are feeling safe and comfortable, not hiding anything from yourself, you can realize there is no point arguing with him now: you cannot reason with anyone who is under stress of a strong emotion, a frightened child or an angry adult. You cannot communicate with a person while he is in the grip of a pseudo-emotion; he does not know what he really feels since he is trying desperately to avoid feeling it, and so he tends to distort your words and misinterpret your intentions. When you are open to your own feelings, not hiding them from yourself, you can accept this other person's right to be irrational once in a while; you will not feel too threatened by his lack of logic. You will be able to respond spontaneously, intuitively, to his hidden message even though he himself may not know exactly what is troubling him. I call this good communication in marriage. The wise husband knows, when his wife bursts into tears in the midst of what he thought was a purely intellectual discussion, that it is time to check the calendar: she is probably suffering premenstrual depression. A wife who knows her husband is having trouble on the job is not too surprised when he growls at the children or complains about her cooking. But suppose she is not aware of any job trouble, can she still accept his irrational behavior? Yes, so long as she is not hiding anything from herself, she can recognize the hidden message behind his actions: she knows he is troubled about something. She does not have to understand him (she is not his psychotherapist) to respond to his hidden need. She can give him permission to be unreasonable, remembering that she is sometimes that way too, and intuitively she will say and do something to reassure him at this moment.

In a good marriage, the partners are rarely irrational *at the same time*: they take turns. Each has vulnerable areas (money, food, sex, success, intellectual ability, recreation can all be contaminated by hidden meanings) but these areas do not overlap each other. For example, if food symbolizes love to the husband, and his wife has no hidden feelings about it, she can comfortably cater to the child within him, and, since she loves him, probably finds this peculiarity rather endearing.

Or if the wife has hidden feelings about money, and her husband is rational about it, he will find a way to solve their financial problems and may even accept her weakness as charmingly feminine.

In a bad marriage, the picture is different. Both partners share too many of the same vulnerable areas: each has his own hidden feelings about the same things; they are irrational at the same time. The husband is finicky about food because it symbolizes love to him (If you loved me you would cater to my tastes) and his wife bursts into tears whenever he criticizes her cooking for the same reason (You are rejecting my love.) Or they both equate money with power: the man doles out a few dollars at a time in order to feel powerful and the wife feels helpless and degraded at her need to ask for money.

How does it feel when you are hiding something from yourself at the same time as the other fellow? It seems to you he is irrational and you cannot stand it. You get involved in long, complicated arguments where neither understands what he himself is feeling underneath, and each misinterprets and distorts the other's words: a complete breakdown in communication. Because you are hiding your real feeling from yourself, you tend to act in a self-defeating way: you say or do the very thing that provokes your partner to hurt you more. Example: the husband says something which threatens to make his wife feel rejected, (an emotion which was appropriate toward her father many years ago). She covers up this feeling with pseudo-anger toward her husband. This anger threatens to make him feel the helplessness which was once appropriate toward his mother in a similar situation when he was little. He covers up his hidden helplessness with pseudo-anger toward his wife. This adds to her hidden feeling of rejection, which she covers up with more anger, and 'round and 'round they go.

I have described the good marriage and the bad marriage. There is the in-between marriage where some irrational areas overlap and some do not. Sometimes these people can accept and respond to each other's hidden needs; sometimes communications break down and they torture themselves and one another. If *one* member of this partnership practices self therapy, matters improve.

Suppose you are married to someone who is generally reasonable, but suddenly he becomes slightly irrational. How can you tell whether or not you too are hiding something from yourself? Here are some clues: 1. You keep trying to explain yourself and you find it impossible to communicate: you cannot get through to him. He seems less intelligent, more stubborn than usual, simply won't listen to reason. You find yourself frantically trying to break through an invisible barrier. No doubt he is irrational now, but so are you. If you were not hiding something from yourself, you would see the whole thing differently. You might a) find another way to approach the problem, b) accept his right to be irrational and leave him alone instead of trying to talk him out of it, or c) realize this message you are so eager to force on him is really not that important after all. (Example of this later.)

2. Your partner is irrational and you can't stand it. It seems too terrible to bear. You want to lean on him the way a child leans on a parent and his momentary weakness is frightening to you.

3. You find yourself thinking obsessively about something this other person did or said. You go on chewing over the same old cud, bored with the monotony of your own thoughts.

4. You feel some emotion too painful to bear, like hating the person you love. (See my experience with Bernie's lunch in "Thinking it Through Alone")

Any one of these clues indicates it is time to explore your apparent emotion. As soon as you can feel the hidden feeling, you will be in the position of the person in a good marriage, who can respond to his partner's need spontaneously, intuitively. When you stop hiding something from yourself, you can overcome the block in communication: you can get through that barrier. The more often you dare to feel your hidden feelings, the more your marriage improves.

Sometimes a student protests, "Self therapy is fine, but how much can I accomplish all by myself? I'm having trouble with my marriage and my husband doesn't believe in the unconscious." It is not absolutely necessary for both members of this partnership to learn self therapy. If only one can look within, tension eases up considerably. When you stop kidding yourself, you find you do not have to make a mountain out of every little molehill: you stop trying to force the other person to be reasonable all the time. When you become aware of your own irrational impulses, when you let yourself hear the child within you, you develop a new tolerance and acceptance of your partner's need to be irrational too, sometimes.

Now you can answer his unspoken message, fill his hidden need more frequently. Instead of adding fuel to the flames, aggravating his hidden anxiety, helplessness, weakness, your warmth and acceptance give him a chance to relax, to build up his self-esteem, to be more like the kind of person you need. (This is one of the main benefits of psychotherapy: the patient outgrows some of his self-doubt and self-hatred simply because the therapist accepts and respects him as a human being despite his problems.) If you want to help someone you love, do not tell him about his hidden feelings: do not interpret for him. You cannot force him to practice self therapy. The only way to help him is to be aware of your own feelings: then you will be open to his message and can give him what he needs for his own emotional growth.

Here is an illustration of the use of self therapy to break through a block in communication in marriage. During a period when the three-year gap between my two daughters was greatest, physically and emotionally, their quarrels inevitably ended with Ann, the younger, in tears of rage. To Bernie they seemed tears of helplessness and he felt compelled to dash to the rescue, furious with Jean, the big sister, no matter who was wrong. Each time this happened I would try frantically to calm Bernie down, to explain, to protect Jean from Daddy's wrath, to be the peace maker. I always failed. The harder I tried, the angrier he grew. He was so unlike himsef, so unreasonabe, I couldn't stand it.

I had "analyzed" Bernie's problem: Ann's tears reminded him of his own childhood when he lacked protection from his older brother. Now he automatically identified with the victim and saw Jean as the aggressor, even though these fights were purely verbal, never physical, as his had been. But this knowledge was no help. I am not his psychotherapist and I could not interpret for him, tell him what his hidden feelings were. There seemed no way I could stop him from acting out his pattern. Whatever I said or did seemed to make things worse.

He and Jeanie would end up yelling at each other until she slammed into her room, crying.

One day, after one of these scenes, I finally noticed some clues indicating I might be hiding something from myself: a) although I thought I understood Bernie, I could not stand his irrational behavior, and b) I could not communicate with him: no matter how I tried I could not make him listen to reason. That was step 1. *Recognize inappropriate reaction.*

Step 2. *Feel the apparent emotion.* With Jeanie's voice still ringing in my ears ("You're always picking on me!") it was easy to feel the old helplessness I always suffered at these times, the sense of inadequacy because I had failed once again to keep the peace.

Step 3. *What else did I feel?* What did I feel when I first heard the girls quarreling and knew Annie would soon be crying and Bernie would flare up? Fear . . . of what? Bernie's anger? No. He doesn't hit Jeanie!

Step 4. *What does this remind me of?* My father's anger. For a moment I relived my childhood fear of Dad's rage. What was I afraid of? He might *stop loving me.* A child of divorce, I never felt safe, never took love for granted. For an instant I felt like that helpless child again.

Step 5. *Look for the pattern.* Then I could see how I had been identifying with Jeanie, fearing Bernie's anger. But her relationship with her father was so different from mine with my father. Her home (and her place in it) was safe. She knew she could count on things going on the same way no matter what happened. And she was not a helpless child as I was, but a big girl in her teens, capable of talking back, of protecting herself vociferously against anything Bernie said. She did not need my protection. Father and daughter shouting at each other was not the most attractive scene in the world, but it was far from tragic. So what if Bernie was unreasonable once in a while? He was a devoted father and it was time she learned to humor him (not tease Annie till she cried) or put up with his outbursts.

The next time the girls quarreled and Annie cried, I knew Bernie would butt in, but I was no longer worried. The old compulsion to keep the peace, to protect them from one another, was gone. I felt Bernie had a perfect right to fly off the handle occasionally and Jean could manage this by herself. I went out of the room and kept quiet. So Bernie yelled and Jeanie slammed her door but this time something new happened. In a little while, Bernie, for the first time, asked me in a troubled voice, "What went wrong?" He meant, was there a better way to handle the situation? He recognized his irrational behavior. Now this was wonderful, because in the past I had always tried to explain things to him (he had misunderstood, it wasn't all Jean's fault, or Jean was wrong but he made her feel so sorry for herself that now she could not see her own fault) but he could never hear me. Whatever I said to him then evidently sounded like, "You are a bad father," and infuriated him further.

Now that I had felt my own hidden fear and was able to accept his need to be irrational, I was no longer trying to run things, no longer acting in a self-defeating way. He could afford to see himself in a clearer light. In answer to his question, I said Jean had not been entirely in the wrong and he had given her a chance to feel sorry for herself instead of ashamed of her part in the quarrel. But she had been difficult all day and he had been too patient with her all along, so it was no wonder he finally flew off the handle; I didn't blame him at all. But Bernie's anger was gone now, so he politely knocked on Jeanie's door, went in to apologize for losing his temper, listened to her side of the story, and peace was established in the family.

Not long afterward, Annie began to catch up to her sister, became articulate and tough enough to outgrow tears in quarreling with her, and that particular problem was resolved. But until that day came, Bernie continued to flare up once in a while, and Jeanie continued to fight back at the top of her lungs. Now I kept hands off and it always ended quickly with no real harm done.

DANGEROUS GAMES IN MARRIAGE

IN PSYCHOANALYSIS, the patient often sees in his analyst some-one from his own past: the rejecting father, the weak, overly-permissive mother, the jealous brother. Without realizing what he is doing, the patient misinterprets words and actions of the therapist ("I know you're angry with me!") and acts in ways to provoke the kind of behavior he has learned to expect. The experienced psychoanalyst is aware of what his patient is trying to do. He resists provocation, does not succumb to the temptation to play the role assigned to him. He helps the patient explore these attitudes and feel what is hidden beneath them (fear of the rejecting father, etc.)

In briefer psychotherapy, the patient often does the same thing, but this behavior is not always discussed and analyzed in the direct style of deep analysis. Here too, however, the therapist refuses to play the game: he does not let himself act like the rejecting father, etc. when the patient expects it. He keeps on being himself, the therapist, not a shadow of the patient's past. This consistency on the doctor's part, this refusal to be manipulated into acting a role from his patient's past despite provocation, is one of the factors that help the patient get better. Even without intellectual understanding of the process, this experience breaks the old pattern, gets him out of his rut, teaches him how to relate to a father figure (or mother, or brother, etc.) in a new way.

This game of mistaken identity is one most of us play in everyday life from time to time. (See my chapter, "The Child Within the Adult" for an example of this.) There are tragic marriages based on just such relationships. Some people go from one marriage to another repeating the same old self-defeating pattern. A woman with a compulsive need to suffer at the hands of a man, may gravitate to a partner with a latent capacity for cruelty. She acts in provocative ways to bring out that trait in him, ends up hating him, and is not aware of her part in the drama; nor does he realize how she has led him on.

If this woman were in psychotherapy, trying to treat her therapist

53

in this way, he would deliberately avoid the trap she was unconsciously setting for him. He might not explore with her the reasons behind her behavior. But even without feeling her hidden emotion, without understanding her pattern, she would begin to get better merely because, for the first time in her life, a man resisted her pattern, refused to play the game. Just having a brand new experience of this kind, with no intellectual awareness of what is happening, can help a person to change, to grow emotionally.

In this way a good friendship or marriage can be therapeutic. Suppose you are unconsciously trying to force another person to be your foil in your old, self-defeating pattern. If you are lucky, he is strong enough to resist your manipulations (he has no hidden feelings in this area). Let us say, for example, you have hidden feelings about power. You act helpless and passive. You have always behaved this way with certain people (who have their own hidden feelings about power) and provoked them to be too domineering, to push you around so you could feel sorry for yourself, repeating some old, unexplored problem from your past. Now you try the same old game with this new person who has no hidden feelings about power and, although he does not understand what is going on, he simply will not play the game. He does not meet your passivity with aggression: he simply keeps on being himself. This new experience is a learning experience for you. On an emotional level, with no intellectual awareness, you begin to evolve a new way to relate to people in this damaged area.

This happened to me, the first year of my marriage. I kept house for my father while Bernie was overseas during the war and Dad and I had money troubles. He would dole out ten dollars to buy groceries, and the arrangement was for me to come back for another ten when that was gone. I knew Dad's tastes: he was set in his ways and there was no variation in my marketing habits from week to week. But every time I came around for that ten dollars Dad was surprised. "Just gave you ten dollars the other day! Where did it go to so soon?" That was just his style as I well knew from years of observation when my stepmother was alive; I should have been able to laugh it off. But it drove me wild. When he wanted to know the cost of oranges or tomatoes (which he ate in all seasons, regardless of price) I could never remember. "What do you mean, you don't know? How can you shop without looking at prices?"

Eventually my inability to quote prices was so maddening to him that I agreed to keep track each day of the money I spent in the different stores. He gave me a little notebook and I really meant to comply. Remember wartime rationing? The long lines in each store (no supermarkets); a quarter pound of precious butter under the counter in one; other epicurean delights in numerous others; different colored "tokens"; a squirming baby on one arm (no shopping carts for babies) whose warm winter clothes required loosening and rebuttoning to avoid perspiration and chill. Change and tokens were too much. I tried, but there was always something missing when I had to account for the ten dollars.

All that year Dad and I played that game. He would nag until I broke down and wept with rage; then he would apologize (of course, he trusted me, knew I wasn't trying to cheat him) and soon the whole thing would begin again.

Then Bernie came home, got a job, and we set up housekeeping on our own like real married people for the first time. I was determined to make this a perfect marriage. When Bernie brought home his first paycheck he asked how I wanted to handle it. I didn't know. I was nervous. Money quarrels in both Dad's marriages haunted me. Bernie made helpful suggestions. "You want to take care of the whole paycheck and give me what I need?" No, I was afraid of all that money. "You want me to give you household money every week? OK. How much will you need?" I didn't know exactly. "Doesn't have to be exact. Just give me a general idea." I couldn't say. "Well, how much did you spend at Dad's each week?" I had no idea. "No idea? You've been keeping house for a year and you have no idea how much you spend?" Bernie was not angry, only incredulous, but I was close to tears (arguing about money so soon: the very thing I dreaded most; the downfall of so many marriages). Desperately I sought a solution, a way to avoid money troubles between us.

Suddenly I had a wonderful idea. "Look," I said happily, "just give me ten dollars, and when that's gone I'll come back for more." Somehow Bernie did not think much of that solution. That was a funny way to run a household. That was out!

"Tell you what," he said at last, "you're afraid to handle money so we'll do it together." And that was what we did. He laid out a series of envelopes and labeled each one milk, rent, gas & electric, etc. "All this is overhead," he explained patiently. "Each week we put the right amount in each: one-fourth of the monthly rent and so forth. Whatever's left over you use for household, miscellaneous and savings. See what you can do, OK?" It was OK. I am naturally frugal despite (or because of?) my irrational fear of money, so we managed nicely. After a few years I could do without those envelopes.

But the funny thing is my basic attitude toward money has not changed. True, I can tighten our belts in lean years and spread out when things ease up, but I still cannot say how much I spend each week. Despite a joint checking account I cannot remember what Bernie's earnings are. I am never quite sure of the price of staples. Despite my irrational pattern, we have never quarreled about money.

Fortunately for both of us, Bernie had no such hidden feelings. Money has no symbolic meaning for him (love, power, etc.) so he could be rational: could calmly accept my need to be irrational. He found a solution. He did not need to humiliate me (did not need to gloat over my stupidity in order to feel clever himself); was not shocked by my infantile behavior (did not feel threatened by my inadequacy); did not act like a superior adult humoring a dim-witted child (did not need to feel strong at my expense). He simply treated this as a problem we two adults could solve together, and so my self-esteem was not damaged and I was able to cooperate. With no awareness of the underlying significance of this problem, Bernie did what a good psychotherapist does: he refused to play my sick game; he would not take on the role of domineering father. He just kept on being himself. This helped me to grow.

I have not changed basically in the money area because I still have not felt my hidden feelings about it, but I can manage our household money wisely despite my handicap. More important, I see now, after twenty years of marriage, how often in those first few years I tried to force Bernie to be the parent (all-wise, all-powerful), to assume full responsibility for decisions that should be shared. Each time he remained steadfastly himself. Eventually I began to outgrow some of my childish need for a relationship where I would be dominated. I began to feel and act more like an adult in a real partnership of equals. I was spared the need to hate a domineering husband, the next stage in that old game. Marriage can be therapeutic.

If you want a technical discussion of gamesmanship in human relations, read *Transactional Analysis in Psychotherapy* by Eric Berne.

HOW TO STOP PLAYING DANGEROUS GAMES

SUPPOSE TWO people are playing the kind of game described in the last chapter: the wife is unconsciously provoking her husband to play a role from her past and he, for hidden reasons of his own, succumbs to the temptation to fit into her self-defeating pattern. Is there any way they can help themselves escape from this destructive pasttime? Yes. If *one* of them can feel his hidden emotion, recognize his pattern, he can change his own behavior and give his partner a chance to grow. In the chapter, "Communication in Marriage," I described the game I played with Bernie: how my attempts to "help" when he scolded Jean only aggravated the situation; how I stopped interfering and how he was then able to stop being angry.

Another story. Jane's husband frequently came home at odd hours. She knew very well his job might delay him, that he could not help being late for supper, and yet, each time it happened she saw red. She would wait on pins and needles for Tom to walk in, and then she would fly into a rage. Tom would stand calmly smoking his pipe until she had spent herself, and somehow his "superior attitude" infuriated her further. This went on for a long time. One evening, as the minutes ticked by and Tom was obviously going to be late again, Jane began to feel the old, familiar anger beginning to mount. This time, the adult part of her, the purely intellectual faculty, observed that she knew darned well he couldn't help it, that she had made a fool of herself once too often, and what was the matter with her? Step 1. *Notice an inappropriate reaction.* She was in the midst of Step 2. *Feel the apparent emotion,* so she deliberately went on to Step 3. *What else did I feel?* How did she feel before the anger began, before she was sure Tom would be late again? She remembered watching the clock, growing tense before there was any proof that he was not coming home on time. That tension—how did it feel? A kind of generalized anxiety, fear of something unknown; anxiety so painful that she has escaped into anger. "What am I afraid of?" she wondered. Step 4. *What does this remind me of?* Suddenly she knew: afraid that Tom might not come home at all; that he might desert her as her first husband had done. She burst into tears; the apparent feeling, anger, was gone. In a little while she calmed down. Step 5. *Look for the pattern.* She saw now that her hidden fear of desertion made her cover up with anger. She realized with horror that this could be a self-fulfilling prophecy: if she continued acting out this pseudo-anger, Tom might eventually get fed up and hate to come home.

Why did Tom stand calmly by while she carried on? The child within him was afraid of this angry woman who was so much like the mother he had feared long ago. The only way he could hide that humiliating fear from himself was to be cold and detached and further madden his wife who felt basically unloved. If he had not been damaged in this area, he might have known how to reassure her of his concern; might have seen through the surface anger to the insecurity beneath and found a way to comfort her. They were both playing a dangerous game, but when one of them dared to feel her hidden feelings, the problem was solved.

Suppose you see the pattern, the dangerous game, but you do not know why you are playing it. Without feeling your hidden emotion, can you stop playing? Not usually. You tend to exchange one game for another unknowingly. For example: Mary had been nagging John for years about putting his dirty clothes in the hamper, but he persisted in dropping socks, shorts, shirts, etc. wherever he stood when undressing. She picked up after him and kept on nagging, resentful and martyred. One day it occurred to her that they were playing a game: she the nagging mother who waited on him hand and foot and John the spoiled child who shut out her voice and got his own way. She made up her mind to stop playing this game. From then on his discarded clothes lay where he dropped them. When he complained about the lack of freshly laundered underwear, she complacently announced that she only washed clothes in the hamper; that the days of picking up after him were over. John was hurt and outraged, but in a little while he caught on, and began to put his dirty clothes away.

Mary was proud of the way she had solved her problem, but I say she merely exchanged one game for another. She used to be the Good Mother, indulgent though complaining; now she was the Bad Mother using discipline and John obliged by being the Good Boy. Sooner or later they would inevitably work themselves around to a Bad Mother game in some other area, so long as both were unaware of this pseudo parent-child relationship. What other solution is there to such a problem? To a wife who has no hidden feelings about this laundry business, this does not really seem like a problem. Many women, strict with their children, can accept a certain amount of sloppiness in their husbands. "What can I do if my mother-in-law didn't teach him to pick up after himself? Too late to bring him up now: I'm not his mother." And these wives are not repelled at having to pick up after one person, do not expect perfection in every trivial aspect of life; the mechanics of life are not that difficult. What about the children? Doesn't it set a bad example? Why should it? It will not if you are honest with them and with yourself. "I didn't bring up Daddy; I'm bringing you up. Lots of things he can do that you can't. He's the daddy and you're a child, so pick up your socks."

When Mary talked about picking up John's dirty clothes, it was obvious that the whole situation had hidden meanings for her. "Who does he think I am," she would mutter irritably, "his servant?" This was a degrading experience for her. If she had dared to explore this apparent feeling and could find what lay underneath she would find a true way to stop playing her dangerous game, instead of exchanging one game for another.

Once I came across a hidden feeling by accident, using the method described in the chapter, "Sneaking up on the Hidden Feeling." I was peeling apples for a pie, listening to a recording of Hungarian folk music, when I suddenly felt like crying. I did not know why. It was happy music, peasant dances. What was bothering me? Years earlier I might have changed the record, but by now I knew I could not waste this opportunity, this feeling which did not involve any personal failure of my own, no guilt or shame or inadequacy to weaken me.

When the record came to an end I played it again and again. The sadness persisted and I asked myself, "What does this remind me of?" Happy peasants dancing, occasionally shouting out snatches of the melody in raucous voices, informal and spontaneous. They seemed to be having such fun. Like a party. Parties . . . I loved parties. Not those huge gatherings of polite strangers making small talk over cocktails, but small, intimate groups of old friends; music and good food and stimulating conversation. Parties where I felt safe among people who knew and liked me; where we were all more attractive and wittier than our everyday selves; where I basked in a magical warmth and hated to leave until the very end.

For years parties had been a sore spot in our marriage. Just as

I loved parties, so did Bernie hate them. We had worked out certain compromises. Sometimes we stayed home and missed a party to please him: then I felt martyred and Bernie felt guilty. Sometimes we went to please me: then I worried because he was bored, and around midnight (when the party was beginning to warm up) he would grow pale and terribly *thin* to my guilty eyes. If I managed to avoid seeing these symptoms of fatigue and stayed very late, Bernie would quietly punish me by catching cold the next day.

What else did this music remind me of? Gypsy music. Hungarian gypsies. My mother's parents came from Hungary! (They did not, as a matter of fact. Where did I get that idea? Perhaps a hidden part of me was trying to help the self therapy process. I have had similar experiences several times.) Gypsies . . . Dad used to refer scornfully to my mother's family as "Bohemians—just like a bunch of gypsies." This made me think of the parties at grandma's house. My first five years, before my parents separated, there were frequent parties in that big, old house; aunts and uncles and cousins and friends of the family, all ages. Marvelous parties: lavish food and laughter and music, singing and dancing. I was the favorite grandchild, petted and made much of, encouraged to show off, dance for the company.

Then the bottom dropped out of my world: My parents separated and I went to live with Dad. He kept me away from "that family." In one clean sweep I lost my mother, my home and *all those parties*. Suddenly, remembering this, I felt like a child again, sobbing bitterly over my terrible loss, furious with Dad who deprived me of all those wonderful parties. (At this moment they seemed more important than anything else I had suffered, the dreadful foster homes, the growing up motherless, etc.) This mood lasted a few seconds. After that the record no longer had the power to move me, no sad overtones; it was just merry dance music. This new knowledge about myself had no practical use for me as far as I could see and I forgot all about it.

About a month later, on a Saturday morning, I begged Bernie to take it easy. "Save your energy today. Remember we're going to that party tonight."

"Party? What party?" With exasperated patience I reminded him of his long-standing promise to attend this particular party. I had been talking about it for days. Was he backing out now? Oh, no, he had every intention of keeping his promise. Just forgot, that's all. So naturally he chose that day to do some really ambitious gardening, including digging an enormous hole to plant a tree. By the time evening came, time to dress up, Bernie was stretched out on the couch in utter exhaustion.

"Party? What party?" he asked in horror. I was ready to explode; so furious I did not trust myself to speak. I rushed off and locked myself in the bathroom. (When in doubt, do nothing and get away from the scene of action fast.) Gazing at my reflection in the mirror for companionship, I began to recount my grievances in a furious whisper. I said exactly what I thought of that monster, raked up frustrations of all the past years, let myself use outrageous adjectives I had never uttered aloud, and was just about to burst into tears when the whole thing began to sound strangely familiar.

Parties . . . my intense love for parties. Suddenly I remembered the Hungarian dance music and how I had cried for my lost child-hood parties, the rage at my father. I did not have to feel those hidden emotions again; it was enough to remember them. And with that memory, the apparent emotion, anger toward Bernie, disappeared. For the first time it occurred to me that it wasn't *this* party I craved: it was those long-ago parties, family parties. It wasn't Bernie who cheated me: it was my poor father who did what he felt was best for me.

And a brand new thought: I can't help being crazy about parties; they have special meanings for me. Bernie hates parties. Maybe they have hidden meanings for him too; maybe he can't help the way he feels any more than I can. Suddenly I knew I did not want to go to this party if Bernie was tired.

I went inside. "Let's go to the movies instead." Bernie likes a good movie and can enjoy it even when he's tired.

"But I thought you had your heart set on this party." He was looking guilty; he knows what it means when I dash off and lock myself in the bathroom like that.

"It's not that important. There'll be other parties." So we went to the movies and I enjoyed myself. For the first time, I had given up a party without feeling deprived and martyred.

There were other parties and sometimes Bernie went. But I began to evolve a new solution to our old problem. Occasionally, when he was too tired, I went all by myself, and found to my surprise, that I could have fun, come home and share all the details with him, and feel less guilt about going without him than I used to feel when he reluctantly dragged himself along for my sake. After a few years,

I noticed myself *losing my old craving* for parties, and now finally I find myself preferring to stay home. Do married people grow more like one another? Or have I simply lost a neurotic symptom which used to disguise my basic similarity to Bernie?

Moral: 1) When you dare to feel your hidden emotions, you can be more accepting of the irrational feelings of the person you love. I am not Bernie's analyst: I do not know why he hates parties, but as soon as I stopped hiding things from myself I could let him feel that way. (Some readers will object that hating parties is perfectly rational. The point is, it seemed irrational to me and I couldn't stand it.)

2) I had been playing a game: acting as if I were completely dependent on Bernie for parties. I could not go without him and I resented the deprivation suffered when I stayed home for his sake. After I felt the hidden feeling (angry with Dad, not Bernie) I could stop playing that game: I could go to parties on my own. After a while, the child within me seemed to lose that old craving and I begin to find I am more like my husband than I ever suspected.

Did I simply switch my anger from Bernie to my father? No. The hidden feeling about childhood, family parties and rage at Dad lasted only a minute, like any hidden feeling. The child within me felt something which to the adult me seems absurd. Usually, after you have felt a hidden feeling you will recognize that it has nothing to do with your everyday intellectual processes, and appears ridiculous as soon as the self therapy experience is over.

HIDDEN FEELINGS IN FRIENDSHIP

LITTLE SUSIE comes home crying and passionately declares, "I'm never going to play with Ellen again!" You breathe a sigh of relief. Ellen has been making Susie miserable for a long time and you have been debating whether or not to put a stop to this painful friendship. But your relief is short-lived: next day the two little girls are chums again and all is forgiven.

What can you do? Nothing. Children make and break friendships from day to day and cannot be expected to abide by their decisions. All you can do is stand by with sympathy when they air their grievances, button your lip when they forgive and forget too easily, and mind your own business. Why can't you help Susie by making a decision for her? For one thing, once you get into the act (breaking up the relationship, forcing Susie to "learn" from your experience) you are denying her the opportunity to learn from her own experience, which is the only way she can learn. Besides, every time you over-ride her right to make her own decisions about people you undermine her confidence in her own judgment; you keep her from growing.

What does Susie see in Ellen? Why does she want her for a friend? You are not Susie's psychoanalyst: you cannot expect to understand everything about her. She is more than an extension of your personality or a piece of clay to be molded. She is an individual in her own right, with needs that she is trying to fulfill in her own way. Respect for the individual means respect for his attempts to help himself and make his own mistakes.

A friend fulfills your child's needs on several levels. Perhaps in your opinion this friend is too young, too passive for your child. But maybe this is a period when your youngster needs to feel older or stronger than another. He may feel inferior to an older brother, or be trying to control his jealousy of the baby. Friendship can provide opportunity for experiences lacking in the family. Remember that your child has his own reasons for his choice of companions, even though some of these reasons may be unconscious. Unless there

63

is real danger, it is best to respect his judgment. Small children need some supervision to protect them from one another, of course, so stick around.

What if your older child is running around with a gang culturally and intellectually inferior to him? What can you do? Not much. A youngster latches on to the crowd that accepts him. If he could get better friends, he would. Criticizing his friends lowers his self-confidence and makes it that much harder for him to graduate from this group to a better one. For an adolescent, remember, inferior friends are better than no friends at all. Sometimes parents need to move to a different neighborhood to get a child out of his rut, away from a really delinquent gang; they may need professional help to discover why their child is going in this direction.

Adults, too, have hidden feelings about their friends. Sometimes this makes good material for self therapy. I had a chance to learn something about myself in this way. When I first came to live in this state, years ago, I felt exiled in a strange land. In my terrible isolation, I was most grateful for the friendship of a most hospitable woman. Margaret wined me and dined me and introduced me to her friends. She chauffered me around (until I learned to drive) to luncheons and shops and was so lavish with her time and energy, so warm and generous, that I began to look on her as the big sister I never had. Partly due to her efforts, I soon found a niche for myself in the community and became less dependent on her practical help; besides, I learned to drive. Nevertheless, when Margaret suddenly dropped me like a hot potato, I was shaken. I forced myself to visit her one day and speak candidly. I said I felt something had gone wrong with our friendship; that perhaps there was some kind of misunderstanding; had I done anything to hurt her? Margaret replied coolly that she had no idea what I meant. It was like a slap in the face and I felt like a fool. I got away as soon as I decently could. But I was miserable. I could not stop thinking about her, which was peculiar since I did not really miss her companionship. Aside from her generosity and my gratitude, we had little in common; I had not originally sought her out as a friend. Still I kept thinking about her in an obsessive way (What happened? What could I have said or done? How could she change like that? Maybe she never did like me—had I imagined it? etc., etc.) This preoccupation with Margaret's defection went on for a long time and Bernie got pretty bored with the same old record. "What difference does it make?" he wanted to know. "She's not your type anyway." I knew he was right and yet I was tormented.

Weeks, months went by, and finally years. Of course I stopped the obsessive thinking and forgot about Margaret after a while. But every once in a while I would hear her name mentioned by a mutual acquaintance and my heart would beat faster, like a girl hearing of an old sweetheart. And sometimes I would run into her at the supermarket. Those were the times I really suffered: my heart beat so loud I feared it might be audible and I had trouble breathing. Each time we would smile pleasantly and exchange greetings (you know how hypocritical women are): how well you're looking and how are the children and I would get away as soon as possible, feeling shaky. Sometimes I could see her at a distance and manage to avoid that painful exchange, but even then I suffered.

One day it finally occurred to me that there was something peculiar about my attitude. That was Step 1. *Notice inappropriate reaction.* I made up my mind to take advantage of the next meeting to *feel the apparent emotion* (Step 2.) and that is what I did. There came a day when I caught a glimpse of Margaret at the supermarket. As usual, the sight of her among the distant cabbages made my heart pound and I had trouble catching my breath. I dashed out to sit alone in my car and *feel.* What was that apparent feeling? I was not quite sure, but the physical symptoms spelled anxiety.

Step 3. *What else did I feel?* I tried to remember what happened years ago when Margaret dropped me. What had I felt then? Shock, surprise, incredulity. I just could not believe that this woman, who had been my devoted protector, could suddenly lose interest in me. She had been so good to me, like a mother.

Step 4. *What does this remind me of?* "Like a mother." That was the key to the hidden feeling. Suddenly I remembered a hidden feeling I had come upon once before in self therapy (crying over a short story and tracking down those tears) about my own mother who had loved me and dropped out of my life when I was five. For a brief moment, the child within me felt a little of that old loss and tears welled up in my eyes. I could remember how I cried last time and this time I did not have to feel it so intensely. It was enough to remember it.

Step 5. *Look for the pattern.* I knew now that I had been feeling all these years as if Margaret were a loving mother, my mother. No wonder I could not forget Margaret's desertion.

Immediately my anxiety symptoms, the apparent emotion, disappeared; I felt fine. After that, I had no more trouble about Margaret. On the rare occasions when we accidentally met in the future I could smile and chat briefly with composure.

Why did Margaret drop me? I do not know. In the early days I used to thrash this out with mutual friends and was told this seemed to be Margaret's pattern: she "rushed" people and later dropped them. I used to wrack my brain trying to "analyze" her, to understand her motivation. But after I knew my own hidden feelings about her I could stop trying to figure her out. That's her problem. I am not her psychotherapist.

A few years later I had another peculiar experience. Jenny and I seemed to have a great deal in common: both had small girls, both enjoyed concerts, lectures and the theatre. Jenny was delighted to find a companion with whom to share her interests and she immediately began to plan all sorts of outings which generally included husbands. In those days I was timid about telling people I was married to a hermit who just wants to stay home with his wife; I tried to compromise. Sometimes I dragged Bernie along to make a foursome, but as time went on I had to make more and more apologies for his absence, and we were a threesome or just two females. Jenny was not happy with these arrangements and sometimes she gave me an odd look when I cautiously suggested about some new proposal (she was full of them) that I didn't think Bernie would want to come along. I do not know what she was thinking, but after a while she dropped me. No more Jenny, I was a little relieved because I hated begging Bernie to join us, and frankly, I was getting a little fatigued myself with all this activity. Jenny and I were still acquaintances, not yet friends. Despite our common interests we were basically a very different in our values and goals. Besides, she seemed so enigmatic: I never managed to penetrate that cool exterior. So I cannot say I was unhappy when the break came; in fact, I took a deep breath and began to relax.

But somehow the whole thing depressed me. Whenever I thought of Jenny I felt sad. If I bumped into her at a concert or lecture I suffered the old anxiety symptoms I used to have about Margaret.

Several years went by and one day, out of a clear sky, Jenny phoned to invite me to her house for a certain cultural activity that was up my alley. My first thought was to refuse politely; I did not want to get involved again. At the same time, I felt a deep urge to see her again. Now I realized that my reaction to her was inappropriate (Step 1.). I wanted to use this opportunity to use self therapy and find out what I was hiding. I asked permission to bring a friend instead of Bernie.

Hilda and I had long been good listeners for one another in self therapy, so I told her all about it and asked her to go to Jenny's house with me and help me explore the problem after our visit. I did not know what my apparent feeling (Step 2.) was, so I planned to deliberately expose myself to an experience which would stir me up, and then follow it up immediately while it was hot off the griddle. So we went to Jenny's that evening and I let myself feel. On the way home I tried to describe my feelings to Hilda. "I felt drawn to Jenny," I began, trying to sort out my reactions. "I was sad, as if I had missed something important, never getting to really know her well. She's so mysterious. Her face is so interesting; don't you think so?" No, Hilda did not think so at all. "But doesn't she seem to be a person who might be fascinating if you could really understand her, really know her?"

"No. I thought she was an oddball," said Hilda in her downright fashion, "but she bored me stiff." I was shocked; Hilda and I usually like the same people.

What was there about Jenny that intrigued me, gave me that sense of loss? Something familiar about that thin face, those grave eyes, that quiet manner. Who did she remind me of? Suddenly it came to me: "Claire. Of course, she reminds me of Claire." I began to tell Hilda about Claire, my first real chum, whom I had loved like a twin sister in my early teens before I was ready for boy friends. Claire and I were inseparable for a few years. Then one fatal summer she went to the country and transferred her affections to another girl, and I was utterly bereaved. I remembered my misery at that desertion. Talking about it now to Hilda, I was able to relive the shock, the incredibility of that experience. "I couldn't believe it. I couldn't understand. How could Claire stop being my best friend all of a sudden?" and I cried a little as if I were that child again. Suddenly those words had a familiar ring: I had cried this way and said these words when I felt the hidden feeling about my mother. Then it was all over. I was grown-up and calm again.

Step 5. *Look for the pattern.* I had been seeing Jenny, not as herself, but as a shadow of Claire whom she faintly resembled. My

67

violent reaction to Claire's desertion must have been a cover for my feelings about my mother.

The mystery of Jenny was solved for me. I could meet her as casually as any former acquaintance, with no heartburnings. Once again I had freed myself from a ghost of the past.

THE IDEALIZED SELF-IMAGE

EACH OF us has a secret picture of himself as he would like to be. This idealized self-image is not completely conscious; in fact it is mostly hidden. Like all hidden feelings it is irrational, exaggerated; it belongs to an earlier, childish level of reasoning. The Absolutely Perfect Parent (whose children are *always* happy), the Absolutely Perfect Wife (who is *never* annoyed at anything her husband does, and shares all his hobbies), the Absolutely Self-Sufficient Adult (dependent on no-one for anything), etc.: all impossible, fantastic standards which the mature mind would find absurd if they were brought out into the open for realistic examination and evaluation. But these self-images are hidden and we unwittingly let them determine our attitudes and actions: we are always trying, in hidden ways, to live up to the inner picture. This, like any hidden motive, leads to trouble. The impossible demands of your self-image frequently conflicts with your other drives. You can even have two conflicting self-images pulling in opposite directions. What happens when your self-image interferes with some other need? You suffer: sometimes a painful apparent emotion like depression or anxiety, sometimes physical symptoms like headache or tension.

The way out of this dilemma? Self therapy: peel away the outside layer and feel what is hidden underneath. Step 5. *Look for the pattern.* It will show you your idealized self-image in all its childish distortion.

You may have these conflicting self-images: the Absolutely Perfect Housewife (loves to stay home, bakes her own bread) versus the Successful Career Woman (made for bigger things and will set the world on fire). One alone can be a strain, but try living up to both of them and you are in trouble. You keep running back and forth from one role to the other and can never reach your goal: to be in both places at the same time. When you discover, through self therapy (or any kind of psychotherapy), just what your idealized self-images are, you get some relief.

Example: One morning when my small daughter missed the bus,

69

I drove her to school. Just as I was about to pull up in front of the building, two adolescent boys strolled directly in front of my car. They seemed so deep in conversation I was afraid they were unaware of their danger, so I blew my horn to warn them. They turned around and laughed in my face, raucous and hostile. My little girl glanced at me in dismay, so I smiled reassuringly and said, "Silly boys." I felt a moment's tension and then thought, "What dreadful experiences these boys must have had all their lives with adults, to make them hate us at sight." Then I drove home and forgot it.

Several hours later, in the midst of household chores, I realized I was mildly depressed. I tried to figure out what was troubling me, but I could not think of a thing. This was a clue I was hiding something from myself: (depression always is). Step 1. *Notice inappropriate reaction.* I phoned a friend, told her I was blue, and invited myself over for a brief visit.

In a little while I was chatting comfortably over a cup of coffee, forgetting the depression that brought me there. Just as the toothache disappears when you get to the dentist, it is deceptively easy to distract yourself from self therapy: you naturally want to put the whole thing off and let sleeping dogs lie. I forced myself to get down to business, knowing the depression would come back later if ignored; described how I felt earlier and soon the depression came back again, That was Step 2. *Feel the apparent emotion.* Step 3. What else did I feel when this began? When did it begin? I began to work backward like a detective. How did I feel when I woke up that morning? Fine. It was only ten a.m. now, so something must have happened this morning to threaten me with a hidden feeling. Anything outside my regular routine? "Drove Jeanie to school, that's all." Did anything unusual happen then? At first I could not remember; then I thought of those boys and their hateful laughter. What did I feel then? A moment of tension. Was there something else I was afraid to feel? Anger? Oh, no, not me. I wasn't like all those prejudiced, ignorant adults who automatically hated the stereotype of the tough teen-ager they feared. Not I; I, who had studied the problems of emotionally deprived adolescents; I, who cared so much about the plight of the potential delinquent and knew so much about his background!

Suddenly I began to cry. In rapid succession I felt two emotions, and both of them made me weep: anger toward those nasty brats and then shame because the anger conflicted with my idealized self image, the Saintly, Understanding Adult who forgives all and is invulnerable to this kind of nastiness. I cried for a few minutes (the shame lasted longer than the anger) and then I was OK. The depression was gone and I was fine for the rest of that day.

Whenever you discover your idealized self-image you realize how fantastic it is, how impossibly high its standards, how frequently you must fall short of it. Does that mean the self-image is a fake? That the Real You is different? No. If you have been trying all your life to be a certain kind of person, then in some part you are. Once you can recognize how unrealistic your goal was, how many opposing drives you have, you will be freer to make voluntary choices. When you feel your hidden feelings, you can more easily act like the person you want to be; much of the time you will choose to go in the direction of that goal. But now, when you occasionally do make a different choice, you need not hate yourself for failing to live up to that old image. You may feel a moment of shame, as I did, but then you can accept the complexity of yourself, rather than act as if you have one simple direction in your life.

Some years ago I used to get regular weekend headaches. Headaches for me are always an indication I am trying not to feel some emotion. I began to track down this inappropriate reaction and this is what I discovered. Five mornings a week I get up early, serve breakfasts at different times like a short-order cook, pack lunches, and in general scurry around uncomplainingly to get my family out on time. But weekends I indulge myself. After breakfast Saturday and Sunday I sit around luxuriously reading. In those days my girls were at the age when they had to come running in and out with problems and conversation and other distractions as soon as Mommy settled down with a book.

Earlier in self therapy I had discovered one of my various idiotic self-images: the Absolutely Perfect Parent. This seemed to mean I must value "togetherness" at any cost: rejoice to have my kiddies gather 'round with their childish prattle, be grateful to have them home in the morning. On the other hand, I am a compulsive reader: I read the way an alcoholic drinks. Deprive me of books and I suffer withdrawal symptoms. To people like us, constant interruptions when lost in the printed page are a form of refined torture. But my idealized self-image, the Absolutely Perfect Parent, forbade me to be annoyed. I never complained, but tore my eyes away from my book every few minutes with a smile and a kind word.

This conflict between my overwhelming craving to read and my need to be the best parent in the world was giving me headaches which lasted all weekend and made me a miserable, crabby mother, not much fun to have around. This is a perfect example of self-defeating behavior.

I did not need self therapy to figure this out, since I had long ago discovered that idealized self-image. All I had to do was put two and two together now and realize how foolish I was. I was then free to use my intelligence (such as it is) and experience to solve my problem.

The next Saturday morning after breakfast I went back to bed with my book. I closed the bedroom door with instructions not to be disturbed except in an emergency. I knew as long as I was away from the center of the house the children would naturally pester Daddy instead of me. For an hour or so I read in peace and comfort; then I was able to give my full attention to the family, with no headache to keep me from being the kind of mother I wanted to be.

I had remembered my idealized self-image, accepted my need to fall short of its standards once in a while, and was then fortified to come closer to that ideal for the rest of the weekend.

A friend of mine was planning to take a vacation trip with her husband and three little boys. "But the baby," she shook her head and sighed, "I don't know how we'll manage with the baby." The baby was adorable and I loved him. But as Mary went on discussing the difficulties of diapers and baby food en route I began to stiffen with alarm. I felt she was trying to tell me something: she wanted me to take the baby off her hands; she was hoping I would suggest it myself and spare her the embarrassment of asking. For a moment the thought of that responsibility, taking complete care of someone else's baby, terrified me. But it seemed to me she *wanted* me to do it, she was willing me to say the word and I could not resist that unspoken demand. Slightly appalled, I heard myself eagerly begging for the privilege of keeping the baby with me, outshouting her protests, insisting what a treat it would be for me.

So I was stuck with a strange baby whose needs I did not understand, who could not tell me what he wanted. "He loves baby food right from the jar. He's happy to stay in the playpen all day. Never needs rocking, sleeps through the night." His mother's words rang hollowly in my ears for the following two weeks. The baby outgrew his regular commercial baby food the second day and it took the whole family's ingenuity and infinite patience to find out by trial and error what he would eat. He began to walk and furiously objected to the prison of his playpen. Since my house was not baby-proofed I had to trot after him all day to protect him from danger. He changed his sleeping habits (naturally, with Mommy gone from his life) and I spent my nights rocking him.

As I groggily rocked him in the middle of a certain dreary night, I caught myself regarding that stubborn little face with rage, and I realized I had been in a state of chronic anger toward his mother for days. It was beginning to spill over on this poor little innocent. What a rotten mother to desert a child this way (I never took vacations when my children were babies); how dare she use me this way (*I* never used people); taking advantage of my generosity (*I* never took advantage of anyone). I was getting angrier and angrier. It occurred to me that when Mary came home I would probably blow up and say horrible things I might later regret. I did not trust myself to face her with all this pent-up fury. I would have to siphon some of it off beforehand.

So the next day I talked with another friend and told her the whole story. She easily sympathized with my wrongs and I managed to let off considerable steam. "But I don't understand," she said. "You say you offered to take the baby before she asked you? Why?" I did not know, but suddenly I saw myself through her eyes and *recognized an inappropriate reaction,* Step 1.

Step 2. *Feel the apparent emotion.* Later, when I was alone, I thought about it some more. How did I feel when Mary first began to talk about her vacation? I thought I could read her mind: she wanted me to take the baby but was afraid to ask for fear I might refuse. I remembered my desire to escape from the whole problem, to avoid getting involved; and conflicting with that was the need to be "good," better than the average person. I not only had to take the baby off her hands, but I also had to spare her the embarrassment of asking for help. I had acted as if she were doing me a favor by letting me have him.

Step 3. *What else did I feel?* A secret hope that no matter how I urged her, she would refuse to give me the baby, that I could make this wonderful gesture and get off paying for it, have my cake and eat it.

Step 4. *What did this remind me of?* I could not think of anything helpful. *What did I seem to be doing?* If I were an outsider, looking on, what might I think of this behavior? I was acting like

73

a generous person, I felt like a generous person, but somehow I was beginning to feel like a fool. There was something compulsive about this generosity, not really spontaneous. I was being good in a way I really did not want to be: taking on a job I dreaded. I seemed to be acting as if I were confused about the meaning of generosity, as if I had no free will.

What else did this remind me of? I tried again, this time going off on a tangent hoping for a new slant. What did I know about the real meaning of generosity? How do we get our first experiences in giving? What does the small child have of his own that he can give? Psychology tells us the child being toilet trained "gives up" his bodily products to please his mother, his first experience in giving. What did that remind me of? Like most parents of my youth, my mother was overly concerned with "regularity": there was a whole daily ritual of examination and discussion about my excreta. Not that she punished me, for failure, but rather rewarded me with great warmth and approval for accomplishment. Then came the loss of my small world: my parents separated and I was boarded out for two years with an eccentric and sadistic foster mother. Among the other bizarre ways of handling me, this peculiar woman forbade me the use of the bathroom. Not that this was such a great physical hardship (we were out in the country and I could always resort to the privacy of the bushes) but to a city-bred child it was painfully embarrassing. More important, I was confused and shocked. Here was a mother figure punishing me for a function that had always brought me praise. It was only a small problem at a time when bigger ones loomed in my life and I had long forgotten it. But now I relived it once again. For a moment I was that miserable, confused little girl again in a world that had suddenly turned topsy-turvy, where the old rules were no longer any guide. Once again I suffered the old humiliating helplessness and surprise.

Step 5. *Look for the pattern.* Now that I had felt that old, hidden feeling, I saw myself in a new light. I recalled other times when I had been what Bernie termed a "good-natured slob," when I had been "generous" in a self-defeating way; the neighbor I disliked and avoided until she fell ill. Then I began bringing over hot cooked meals twice daily and somehow found myself continuing with this Lady Bountiful act long after she recovered. She calmly lounged around while I felt like a fool and had all kinds of difficulty putting an end to my servitude. I could remember other, similar situations where I had ended up feeling humiliated and exploited.

I could see my pattern now. I had an idealized self-image of myself as a giving person, one who *always* felt generous, who could never have an ungenerous thought. Whenever I felt ungiving (I was afraid to take care of that baby; I hated feeding a neighbor I disliked) I quickly covered up that hidden feeling with a strong urge to *do* something generous, to prove to myself (and others) what a wonderful person I am. I could remember now the look of genuine surprise on the face of the baby's mother when I insisted on taking him. It occurred to me for the first time that perhaps she had not been hinting; maybe she had never intended to "use" me. It was I, myself, who forced the issue. I had been so frightened by my ungenerous attitude that I rushed into impulsive action to cover it up.

By the time Mary came home from her vacation my anger was almost gone. I could laugh about some of the unexpected problems that had come up in her absence and avoid the terrible scene which would have made us both miserable. We could still be friends.

After that, I learned to keep careful watch over my compulsive generosity. For instance, a neighbor phoned one day to ask if I would drive her and her little girl to the doctor. My first reaction was to accept graciously. When she asked, "Are you sure it won't inconvenience you?" I was all ready to insist I had nothing better to do. But I remembered my old hidden feeling and began to pay attention to how I really felt now. I dared to think some ungenerous thoughts (Why doesn't she learn to drive? How long must her neighbors chauffeur her around? Besides, she can afford a taxi. Her doctor is far away and this will mean hours out of my day.) All this took but a second to think about and with an almost imperceptible pause I was able to politely refuse and tell her about my heavy agenda for the day. She accepted this gracefully; I was only one person on her list of chauffeurs and she did not seem to hold it against me. Of course I felt I had done an outrageous thing, but I felt fine, not even a twinge of guilt. You do not know how much your idealized image will let you get away with unless you test it out.

I still have trouble with that old tendency, occasionally find myself acting out the old pattern, but I remind myself how dangerous it is to pretend to be better than I am and I get out from under once again. In this way I avoid having to feel exploited and hating people. It is painful to hate people if you think of yourself as generous: you're supposed to be loving them all the time; so compulsive generosity can be very self-defeating.

75

THE CHILD WITHIN THE ADULT

THERE IS a part of each of us that still feels like a child, with childlike needs and cravings. If you keep that child hidden, if you cannot learn what it wants, it will trick you into foolish, self-defeating behavior. This child is a part of you that never got what it needed long ago, and never learned how to get it. It makes you do things that frustrate its needs and aggravate the old craving.

One summer I went back to college to take some graduate courses. One was taught by a young man whose manner was outrageously insolent. We were a class of teachers, principals, school supervisors; most of us older than this young whippersnapper. You can imagine how we boiled and seethed all summer, partly in righteous indignation, largely to hide from ourselves the degradation of this regression to elementary school status, after all those years bossing kids around. When the term was over, we got together to sign a letter of complaint, addressed to the Dean of Education. I must point out that my anger seemed perfectly appropriate: I was not alone; almost the entire class signed. It did not occur to me then that it was odd for me to assume leadership: *I* took it upon myself to deliver the letter together with a few thousand well-chosen words. The Dean was agreeably dismayed and apologetic; I went home with a fine feeling of accomplishment.

But somehow I could not stop being angry. Final exams were coming and I could not cram: too busy hating the teacher. I could not concentrate on anything but this dreadful little man. After an entire summer, I was still chewing the same old cud more furiously than ever.

One night I lay tossing and turning, recounting every horrible thing he had said and done. Gradually it dawned on me there might be something wrong with this picture. Granted, the whole class was angry, but surely they weren't all lying awake being angry. (Step 1. *Recognize inappropriate reaction.*) At which point I told poor Bernie (who was just dozing off) I had to talk about this problem. He listened patiently for a while and then tried to persuade me there was nothing inappropriate about my anger. "I don't know why you took that guff all summer," he complained. "Should have walked out the first day!" Often, when you are thinking out loud in self therapy, your apparent emotion may look completely reasonable to the other fellow. Only you yourself can recognize that although this feeling may be appropriate in *kind* it is inappropriate in *degree;* you are over-reacting. So I took time out to explain why I needed to explore this anger.

Step 2. *Feel the apparent emotion.* I went over some of the teacher's more outrageous behavior in order to warm up. When I was as furious as possible I was ready for

Step 3. What else did I feel at the beginning of the term, before my anger reached such proportions? Disappointment, disillusionment. Teaching, to me, is a sacred profession and I hated seeing him fall so far below my standard.

Step 4. What does this remind me of? I thought for a while. Then it occurred to me, for the first time in my life, that I had been through this before. I had felt this disappointment, disillusionment and anger with other men in similar positions of authority: certain employers for instance. "That's funny," I told Bernie, "I'm not the kind of person who judges others. I don't expect people to have my personal values: I'm used to people being different. As a matter of fact, I'm very accepting and tolerant. Why am I so harsh with these— these father figures?"

That phrase, "father figures," just slipped out, and I was surprised to hear it. How absurd! This teacher was years younger than I. But I knew from experience I could not afford to ignore clues that pop out from hiding like that. Alright then, I would follow that clue. What about my feelings toward my father? When I was a child I thought he was a god: omniscient and omnipotent. It was not until I wanted to get married that I finally arrived belatedly at that vital task of adolescence I had skipped: to see one's parents as merely human with human flaws. How did I feel then? Bernie was a wartime soldier and Dad was lonely after my stepmother's recent death. He fought a bitter fight to keep me home with him until "after the war." My disillusionment and rage at his selfishness was a little irrational. Why was I so horrified? No doubt a belated adolescence after too prolonged childhood idolatry is always painful. Perhaps I had to hate my father for a while in order to free myself from him and get married. I do not know; I am not my own psychoanalyst.

77

"What are my feelings toward Dad now?" I took stock. The old anger had disappeared long ago and I felt I loved my father as any normal person does. But, come to think of it, I did have some peculiar attitudes. We were a continent apart now and I wrote letters to him in a compulsive way. I felt driven to sit right down and answer each of his letters the very moment they came. It did not matter how inconvenient it was. Also, whenever anything good happened to us (Bernie's raise, some small recognition of my own work) I could hardly wait to write and tell Dad. Then I would wait, on pins and needles, for his reply, which was inevitably a bitter disappointment; never the special word of praise I craved, never unmitigated approval. This was the first time I ever realized how peculiar, how childish, my attitude was; the first time I really noticed what I was doing.

"What do I seem to be doing?" I thought about this term. Suddenly I saw myself. From the beginning of the summer I had been acting in a nasty, provocative way, designed to infuriate the teacher: criticizing the course outline, sneering at the subject matter, complaining about assignments and meaningless "busy work"; conspicuously smart-alecky. I made a real pest of myself and the teacher hated my guts.

Now I began to cry like a child, hurt because the teacher didn't like me! This was the hidden feeling, and what a horrid surprise: I felt like a fool. Imagine wanting this horrible man to like me! And if that was what I really wanted, why be so dopey as to go out of my way to make him hate me?

Step 5. *Look for the pattern.* I had acted like a bad child who needs approval but does not know how to get it. He makes a pest of himself: the only way he knows to get attention. The child within me craved recognition and approval. Because I was hiding something from myself my behavior was self-defeating. Instead of approval I got the wrong kind of recognition: rejection. I wanted to be the favorite child, teacher's pet, and I became a thorn in his side, a general nuisance.

For the first time in my life, I could look back and see a whole series of relationships just like this: teachers, bosses, men in authority toward whom I had behaved in that obnoxious, provocative way, forcing them to notice me and to reject me. (To know me is to hate me.) And after each rejection I suffered; sometimes obsessional anger, as now; sometimes depression; all because I never knew the child within me was starved for approval.

78

What happened after I felt the hidden feeling and understood my pattern? First of all, I could rest: I stopped thinking about that man and had a good night's sleep. Next day I was able to get on with the business of living and think about other things, free of that boring obsession.

About a month later I noticed that I had outgrown my compulsive correspondence with my father. I was able to answer his letters at my leisure, sometimes forgetting, just as I do with my friends.

Now that I knew my pattern, I was predictable to myself. I could expect to react to some father figure again with the old childish craving, disguised with self-defeating, provocative behavior. Sure enough, about a year later I became involved with an authority figure who finally was so unkind that I came home and wept all day. Finally, toward the end of a grueling afternoon, I began to recognize something familiar about the whole thing. Suddenly I remembered the hidden feeling about my teacher, and lo and behold, the past few months became clear to me: I realized that I had been acting like a pesty child again. This man, of whom I ostensibly disapproved, whom I disliked intensely, was in the position of a father to me, and evidently the child within was going through the same old pattern again. Now that I saw what I had been doing, I knew that my tears were those of that rejected child. With that understanding my whole mood lightened. The drama was over; I could snap out of it and go on living as an adult.

Later, I experimented and found that I could not have any sane relationship with this man: as soon as I came near him, I could feel that old childish need to make him notice me, together with some anxiety symptoms. Sometimes you gravitate toward a person who has, for hidden reasons of his own, the ability to fit in too well with your own irrational needs. In this case, discretion was the better part of valor: I avoided him from then on.

About two years later, the problem cropped up again, but this time I was forewarned by a peculiar clue. One Sabbath in the synagogue, absorbed in the rabbi's sermon, it suddenly dawned on me that he looked like my father. I whispered my discovery to Bernie but he only laughed. "Absolutely no resemblance!" I turned to my daughters. Didn't the rabbi look just like Grandpa? They couldn't see it either.

The dismal truth was I was having some kind of hallucination. What did it mean? I knew darn well what it meant. This time I had no trouble recalling my old trouble with father figures: I would have to watch my step. I had plenty of opportunity for self-observation, since I sang in the choir and the rabbi attended all rehearsals. Little by little, I noticed my urge to act like his favorite child: to ask "interesting" questions about the history of liturgical music (he was a learned musicologist), to worry about his tendency to catch cold ("Have you got your rubbers, Rabbi?"), to tell him how fascinating his sermon was, etc. But I was predictable to myself now, and had a measure of control over myself. I knew I had a choice: I could quit the choir and avoid close association with its temptations, or stick around a while and see if I could deliberately, consciously, avoid making a fool of myself.

This time I was brave and chose to hang on and see what happened. It was an experiment; I could always quit when and if things got out of hand. I am glad to report that I actually was able to "transcend my neurosis" as Victor Frankl says (*From Death Camp to Existentialism* and *The Doctor and the Soul*). Constantly reminding myself of the child within and its craving for approval and special recognition, the adult part of me was capable of keeping my big mouth shut and my intellect could guide my actions. I sang in that choir for two years without making a fool of myself. The rabbi did not have to reject me.

A childish craving which is hidden traps you into self-defeating behavior which adds to that craving, makes it worse. In the old days, before I knew what I wanted from father figures, I kept on provoking them to reject me. Each rejection, each painful experience, further frustrated the child within me, made the deprivation more intense. A hidden craving is irrational: it derives from an earlier period in your life, functions on a different level from your adult self and has no real place in your present life. It is insatiable, that child within you. My desire for the special approval given to a precocious child cannot be satisfied in my adult life. The best we can do with these archaic desires, irrelevant to daily living, is avoid frustrating them. I could not be the rabbi's favorite child, but I could at least spare myself the torment of his rejection and the humiliation of watching myself act like a fool.

A few years later I had the identical warning. This time, the new rabbi was a young man. Once again, in the midst of a sermon it occurred to me that he looked just like an old snapshot of my father when he was that age. As soon as I reached home I dug up that picture and checked with the family. And once again no one saw the resemblance but me. Bernie laughed and I could not blame him: there I was back in the same old rut.

I tried to look back on the past few months. Sure enough, I had been getting involved in long, fascinating, intellectual discussions with the rabbi, showing him how clever I was, how sensitive, how spiritual, etc. etc. ad nauseam. But it had not been going on very long. This time I had caught myself sooner than ever before in this pattern. Now I was able to curb myself, keep that hidden child from pushing me into self-defeating behavior.

Will I have to live with this all my life? When I am a doddering old lady will I still react to some man (young enough to be my grandson) as to a father? Still have to watch myself carefully to keep from playing the fool? Who knows? I am not my own psychotherapist. All I can do is take one step at a time. But note that I had to feel the hidden emotion only once, exploring my anger toward that teacher. It took me that entire summer to recognize that inappropriate reaction. After that, all I had to do was remember it intellectually, not feel it. And each time, I noticed the inappropriate reaction sooner and sooner. With the past two experiences I managed to stop myself *before* fulfilling my old self-defeating pattern: I did not force those two men to reject me. The goal of self therapy is to act like an adult when you are feeling like a child.

In recent years I find myself forgetting to include vital information in my letters to my father (Bernie's raise, etc.) which I used to send to him so compulsively. And one day Dad wrote such a lovely, warm letter of praise for some accomplishment of mine that tears came to my eyes, remembering the old frustration. Has my father changed? Have I learned to communicate to him in a different way, one which makes it easier for him to give me approval? Or was the approval there before, but I unable to see it while the child within me made inordinate demands? I don't know.

HOW TO FREE YOUR NATURAL CREATIVITY

WHEN YOU were very young, before you could speak, you thought in a different way from the way you do now as an adult. Perhaps you recall a little of that old way. Can you remember when you were not too sure of the difference between the animate and the inanimate? When you had a sneaking suspicion that the eyes of the portrait on the wall were watching you? When you found it hard to believe your doll could not feel pain? Harry Stack Sullivan, studying the schizophrenic, learned something about the thought processes of the small child. Did you ever wake in the middle of the night and find it hard to throw off a particularly vivid dream? You found yourself thinking in an irrational way, unable for a minute or two to distinguish dream from reality. This is a sample of the way you once thought, long ago.

Learning to get along with people, to live in the real world, changes the child's thought processes. As soon as parents begin to make demands on the child (toilet training, obedience) he becomes alert to signs of their approval or disapproval. His security depends on knowing what will please Mommy, how far he can satisfy his need to experiment and explore without arousing more disapproval than he can afford. As he matures, the approval of others becomes important, and eventually he develops personal goals of achievement and success.

These kinds of preoccupations with accomplishment and recognition narrow down his awareness. In growing into a practical, realistic person he learns to ignore all kinds of things which absorbed his interest in early childhood; he simply does not notice them any more. They are not important because they are not useful.

Something else contributes to this change in thinking. If you have a small child you will notice that when he first begins to speak he uses words in his own special way; they have a different meaning for him: he is not really communicating yet. After a while he learns that the purpose of speech is communication; but the earlier form of thinking involves ideas that cannot be put into words, that cannot be communicated. He is made to feel that if a thought cannot be made intelligible to another it is not worth having. As he masters the language, he begins to think in words; he limits his thoughts to those which can be verbalized. He stops thinking in the old, primitive way and narrows himself down to the new way.

However, that old way of thinking is not completely lost; it is only kept outside of awareness. In dreams as well as in moments of reverie (when you are lost to your surroundings) you are using that earlier thought process. Certain kinds of problems, which we cannot solve on a direct, intellectual level, are worked out in sleep and in reverie. Lawrence S. Kubie (*Neurotic Distortion of the Creative Process*) calls this earlier style of thinking (which persists in adult life outside of awareness) the preconscious. This is the way you function during any creative activity. Talent, that special gift of the fortunate few, when combined with the free use of the preconscious, produces genuine art. The talented person who is too rigid, too fearful of his irrational (non-intellectual) tendencies, closes the door to that earlier productive kind of thinking. Also, the artist who has too many unresolved problems, too many hidden feelings, compulsively writes the same kind of book or paints the same kind of picture over and over again; is unable to grow in his work unless he can bring the hidden material out into the light of his conscious feeling.

The trouble with talent is the responsibility to make the most of it. Our success-ridden culture puts so much emphasis on getting ahead, acquiring money and/or status, that our feelings about our talents are often contaminated by fear of failure or dreams of glory.

Abraham H. Maslow (*Toward a Psychology of Being*) points out that although few of us are talented, we all have the potential for creativity, if we can only free it. Several years ago it occurred to me that we should experiment with artistic activities in which we have no talent: areas which have not been contaminated by concepts of success and failure, where we have few fears or specific goals. In growing up we join the rat race for achievement (sometimes called "adjusting to reality") and become so preoccupied with goals that we lose the childlike ability to enjoy the process, as Alan Watts points out in his books on Zen.

If you try doing something for which you are convinced you have no talent, you will not expect much from yourself. You will be able to concentrate on the process, the activity for its own sake. (Watch a child at play: it is fun to make mud pies even if no one sees them, buys them, eats them.) You will be able to forget about the end product. When you can lose yourself in the process, you naturally use that earlier, pre-intellectual kind of thinking: you are being creative. Joyce Cary's novel, *The Horse's Mouth*, is a vivid picture of the artist lost in the joy of the process for its own sake.

I have been experimenting with this approach for several years. First I tried modern interpretive dancing, with no real training. Each morning, when the family was gone and I had the privacy I needed (even the cat embarrassed me a little), I kicked off my shoes and danced to the recordplayer: symphony, jazz, whatever fitted my mood. I did not worry about form: I was dancing for myself.

I discovered that twenty minutes of dancing was a fine way to start the day: I was full of pep and enjoyed my housework. "Good for the circulation," was the way I explained it to myself. Then I began to experiment with another activity for which I have no talent, drawing. One morning, as soon as the family had gone, I assembled a few simple household objects: a bowl, a glass, a pitcher, and started on my first Still Life. My small daughter later demonstrated how a gifted person can do this in a few minutes; it took me an entire morning. I had no faith in my fingers so I dared not deviate one iota from the objects in front of me, and slavishly studied every curve and angle. For hours I crouched over the kitchen table in my near-sighted way; poring over the paper, examining and re-examining the bowl, the glass, the pitcher; erasing, drawing, erasing again. With no preconceived expectations, no goals to strive for, I lost myself completely in the task at hand, absorbed in the process for its own sake. For a verbally-minded person like me, it was a new experience to *see* anything so vividly: I had never used my eyes for this kind of observation before, at least not as an adult, and it took a great deal of concentration.

Finally I was done. This was the best I could do, and although my best was none too good, I was not disappointed; in fact I was pleasantly surprised. I glanced at the clock. Good grief! Twelve noon and there were breakfast dishes in the sink, beds unmade. Where had the morning gone? There was a moment of dread as I waited for the guilt, the penalty for those "wasted" hours, to hit me; but oddly enough I felt free and happy as a child. Despite those cramped hours bent over the kitchen table, I felt invigorated, stimulated *just as after dancing*. Household tasks seemed pleasant, easy; I caught up to my schedule with very little trouble.

A little later I noticed something else. I had been suffering from tension in my jaws for several days: something was bothering me but I could not figure out what it was. Now that tension was gone. Somewhere during that morning's art session I had discarded it. While I was busy with the shape and size of things, lost to the practical aspects of "real" life, some other mode of thought process was going on, solving my hidden problem.

Later I went on to painting with water color and oil. For a long time I cautiously pencilled-in my picture before daring to take up the brush. At last I produced a Still Life that satisfied me and then I grew bolder. I dared to discard the pencil and use paint directly; and I decided to paint something out of my own head instead of copying things. The first attempt was a hideous, dead, flat landscape which seemed to reveal how fearful I was of this new freedom. Then I went on to paint waves. I wanted a wild, angry sea but the first few persisted in turning out delicate and stylized. I did not paint regularly; I would pack my picture away and forget it, and go back to do another perhaps once every month or two. Years later, when I dug them all up I was surprised to see that I had been painting seascapes over and over again throughout those many months. Eventually I managed (dared?) to create one dark and threatening enough to satisfy me; next was a calm ocean after the storm, and then I turned to non-representational art.

It is hard to portray reality without talent, so I thought it would be easy to just let myself go and fool around with abstract designs, modern non-objective art. Strangely enough, it was the most difficult task of all. What courage it required to attack that virgin page with the brush when I had no definite picture in mind. What was I afraid of? That something hidden might pop out? I don't know. I only know I sweated out a few of these and then I stopped painting altogether. Had this art form become too loaded with hidden meanings for me? Was I afraid of the freedom of abstract art? I am not my own psychoanalyst; I only know that years later, in a lecture on creativity, when I showed my class these old paintings (to indicate that anything worth doing is worth doing badly), my students pointed out something I had never noticed: all the "non-objective" paintings were really wild waves. It was not until much later, pursuing a different clue in self therapy, that I discovered the hidden meaning of waves for me, and the reason for my preoccupation with them. I think the painting paved the way for that insight. This was an example of the kind of thing Kubie discusses: the artist who gets stuck at one point in his career and unwittingly keeps on painting the same picture, writing the same book. It is poor art but good therapy.

During that year I found a practical use for this kind of activity. One Saturday morning my family was getting on my nerves. After an hour of nagging and scolding, it occurred to me that maybe I was just cranky and irritable. I shut myself in my bedroom with orders not to be disturbed except in emergency, and started to paint. This was during my Still Life period and for a solid hour I worked hard studying the shape of a lamp and a dish, trying desperately to get them down on paper, lost in the process. Then I came back to daily life, went inside to join my long-suffering family and found them lovable and fun to have around: my crabbiness had disappeared and I was a good Mommy again.

Later I tried music. Singing has too many hidden meanings for me, but a musical instrument is a good, non-talented, uncontaminated field for me. I taught myself a few chords on the guitar. It was hard and not much fun; I was all thumbs; but I learned that fifteen minutes with the guitar could ease the old, painful tension in my jaws when something hidden was troubling me and I could not bring it out into the open. The utter concentration required for the difficult task of playing the guitar seemed to take me out of my world, and when I came back fifteen minutes later, some problem seemed resolved outside of awareness. Then I went back to the piano. A few years of childhood lessons have left me with the ability to read notes, but little else; I have to work hard to learn a simple piece. I found I could avoid an oncoming headache with twenty minutes of hard, unremitting piano work. Several times I waked with a full-blown headache and cured it with half an hour's practice immediately after breakfast. The trick is to work hard, not just fool around with easy pieces. Apparently, only when intense concentration is used, can the adult intellectual processes relax and the earlier, primitive thinking function.

One of my students is a commercial artist. One day she was trying to meet a deadline, pretty pictures for a children's storybook. Her creative juices seemed to dry up and the precious minutes were ticking by. She took time out for an activity uncontaminated by goals and standards: dancing. For a few minutes she danced an angry, "ugly" dance, expressing feelings which could not be used in her illustrations.

Then she sat down to work again and the ideas flowed as if from an untapped reservoir. She had freed the creativity within her.

Maslow describes the way some people, without any artistic talent, live their lives creatively: the housewife who creates a warm, beautiful home, the craftsman who enjoys the process of his work and does a satisfying job. My experience indicates that if I take time out once in a while to indulge in some artistic activity for which I have no talent and lose myself in the process, I then go back to the mechanics of living with new zest, an approach that Maslow would call creative.

ANXIETY AND FEAR

YOU KNOW what fear is like: the sinking sensation in the stomach, the cold sweat, the trouble breathing, the palpitations. Anxiety feels just like that. The difference is that with fear you know what you are afraid of; anxiety is a vague feeling: you do not know what you are afraid of. Of course, some of us are so adept at kidding ourselves, at avoiding unpleasant emotions, that we do not even recognize anxiety. When you have all or some of the above-mentioned physical symptoms, presumably without reason, remind yourself that you are suffering anxiety.

We tend to think of fear as normal and anxiety neurotic, but this is untrue. There is normal (real) fear and neurotic (irrational) fear; there is also normal anxiety and neurotic anxiety. I will discuss all four.

How does the pattern for anxiety begin in early life? Different psychoanalysts have differing theories. Harry Stack Sullivan believes it starts when the infant's first feelings of omnipotence (I cry and milk magically appears) give way to the realization of his utter dependency. Then two factors can set the anxiety pattern for life: a) threat of loss of parental love, and b) intense emotion (like rage) while he is developmentally too young to cope with it.

Karen Horney says children in our culture are so dependent on their parents that they cannot afford to feel all the anger and hatred appropriate to the frustrations of daily life. (If I hate Mommy she will hate me.) She says the conflict between dependency and hostility causes anxiety.

Frieda Fromm-Reichman observes that the neurotic's self-esteem is continually threatened by his constant failures due to his self-defeating behavior. She believes this is the basic cause for anxiety.

Rollo May believes every time you strike out in some new path, forge ahead into new channels of endeavor, the child within you feels guilt and disloyalty to your mother, and you suffer anxiety. The more creative you are, the more anxiety you must endure. Rollo May, in *The Meaning of Anxiety*, sums up various schools of thought about anxiety and fear, and concludes that anxiety in adult life always occurs when the basic orientation to life is threatened. Each of us has a deep conviction about what the world is like and what his place is in it. When something happens to violently shake that inner belief we suffer anxiety.

The depression of the nineteen-thirties is a good example. It has long been understood that the conscientious, hard-working American can earn a living: during the depression decent men lost their jobs and could not make an honest dollar. It was a deeply ingrained belief that in this land of opportunity, the man who got rich through his own efforts was secure and he could look forward to greater successes: in 1929 wealthy men lost everything. The shock of this new reality, the failure of the economic system, where the world as men knew it turned topsy-turvy, provoked *real, normal anxiety* all over the country.

But the man to whom material possessions and status represented his whole identity, his sole meaning in life, the man to whom financial failure was a psychological death, suffered *neurotic anxiety*. He was the financier who jumped out of his office window.

Fritz Redl, in his work with disturbed boys, *Children Who Hate* and *Controls From Within*) found that love and kindness aroused neurotic anxiety in these youngsters who had built up a philosophy based on the brutality of their parents, the rejecting, cruel world they knew: "Adults are rotten."

What about real and neurotic fear? I think today fear of atomic warfare is *real and normal*. Real fear makes you do something to relieve the feeling. You write a letter to a congressman or join a peace organization or study research on alternatives to war; then you find this action, no matter how small, gives at least temporary relief from the fear. (Of course people all around us are covering up this fear with apparent emotions like boredom, restlessness, craving for entertainment or tranquilizers.)

On the other hand, I met a woman who was suffering from obsessive fear of atomic war. She confided that she carried around little pills of instant death for herself and children in case of a bomb; could not enjoy anything (life is so temporary); and was doing absolutely nothing to help in the anti-war movement (I feel so helpless). This is *neurotic fear*, a cover for something else. This lady had never enjoyed parenthood because of her obsessive fears about her childrens' health. This kind of person finds an intense, all-absorbing fear from time to time in his life, to hide a deeper anxiety which he has not yet explored and faced.

Phobia is a neurotic fear used to cover anxiety. A phobia is a fear which the person himself realizes is irrational, and yet he has no control over it. Freud's classic study of Little Hans tells of a child's horse phobia (in a period when you could not step outside your front door if you were afraid of horses). Psychoanalysis showed that the irrational fear of horses covered a deeper anxiety about his father whom the little boy loved and feared.

The fear of the dark so common in two-year-olds appears to be a cover for a generalized anxiety typical of this period when he is learning to get along with other children, when his parents are beginning to be less accepting and more demanding (toilet training, obedience), and when he is becoming more sophisticated and aware of danger in his world. The child can be conditioned out of this fear but he will then develop some other cover to disguise the hidden anxiety, and the new defense may be harder to live with than fear of the dark. Better to respect the child's feelings, provide a night light to tide him over this tough period, and have faith that this too will pass.

What can you do with fear and anxiety, real or irrational, normal or neurotic? Feel them. Face them openly and then you will have some measure of control over your actions. It is *hidden* fear and anxiety that give us trouble. The brave man is one who lets himself feel fear when in danger, then uses his head to act wisely. He who hides fear from himself often covers it up with inappropriate, self-defeating behavior, impulsive dangerous actions. Part of the definition of mental health is the ability to tolerate anxiety. The neurotic suffers all kinds of painful pseudo-emotions and/or physical symptoms (headache, psychosomatic illness) to avoid feeling anxiety. The delinquent, on the other hand, rushes into impulsive action to avoid anxiety. He projects his inner conflicts out into the environment, preferring to fight with the outside world rather than feel his own emotions.

Sometimes, if you dare to feel anxiety (or fear) which you know is irrational, you can go on to explore the hidden feeling it covers. Remember that every self therapy experience has to begin with an apparent emotion. Each time you avoid fear or anxiety, you may be missing an opportunity to peel away a layer and learn something new. This does not mean we can always afford to feel fear or anxiety. There are times when we do not have the emotional stamina for such an ordeal. When I have had a bad day and my self-esteem is low I may have to avoid pain; I cannot afford to feel fear or anxiety in full strength and I cannot practice self therapy. Instead, I choose some form of escape: a cheerful book or movie, an ice-cream soda, a shopping spree. Do not scorn such escapes. Few of us are so strong that we never need resort to them. But it is wise, when you are drowning your anxiety in a hot fudge sundae, to realize that this respite is only temporary: the anxiety will come back another time. Think of it as homework which you are postponing for another day; sometime soon, when you are braver, you will dare to feel the anxiety and explore it further if possible.

Suppose you dare to feel the apparent emotion, anxiety or fear, and cannot go on to the other steps in self therapy, cannot find the hidden feeling. It still pays to feel that surface feeling. The chapter, "How to Safely Feel a 'Dangerous' Emotion," discusses this in more detail. You will find there the story of the student who had been avoiding fear in an attempt to be brave. Only after she dared feel the fear was she able to act courageously in a difficult situation. In that chapter I also tell about my sailing experiences. I had been swallowing down my fear of the water for a long time. After I let myself feel it, I finally learned to enjoy sailing. Then, when I had faced the fear, I was able to peel away one more layer with self therapy, discover something new. Sitting on the deck, watching the waves, I asked myself, "What am I really afraid of?" Not drowning: I wear a life-jacket, the boat will not sink if overturned, there are plenty of other boats around to rescue us. Getting wet? The water was warm. Then what? I looked deeper into those wild waves and let that fear wash over me again. What else did I feel? A thrill of excitement. What did this remind me of? Wild waves . . . wild feelings! that's what they meant to me, anxiety about dangerous emotions. Fear of the water was a cover for anxiety about feelings, my own hidden feelings. (The chapter on creativity describes my obsessive preoccupation with waves in painting. Using art, a non-intellectual process, helped pave the way for this conscious awareness of the meaning of waves for me, and a few years later I peeled away further layers, but that is a story for another book.)

One morning I began to notice that I had been mildly depressed for several days. Not the deep depression of my pre-self therapy days, but a general discontent, dissatisfaction with the day's program, boredom with regular chores, inability to look forward to anything pleasant. I knew this meant I was hiding something from myself, and I tried to track this mood to its source. It had been going on for almost a week. What was new in my life this week? At first I could think of nothing, but after a while it occurred to me that Bernie had been talking about his work, something he rarely does. He was getting restless, bored with the job, dissatisfied with a co-worker: all signs that he was getting ready to change jobs although he had not yet said so and I had *not allowed myself to think about it.* My hidden feeling was anxiety at the thought that Bernie might quit his job and begin looking for another, or vice-versa. The painful anxiety lasted a few minutes. Then I could see my pattern: every time I am faced with a change in my life (marriage, childbirth, moving) I am threatened with anxiety. Sometimes I have not been able to avoid feeling anxiety, but other times I cover it up, as I had been doing now, with depression. As soon as I felt the hidden anxiety the depression lifted: I had a happy day. Later, when Bernie was ready to talk over the pros and cons of changing jobs, I was able to transcend my neurosis, as Victor Frankl says, and listen calmly (instead of bursting into tears as if the end of the world was imminent), encouraging him to analyze both sides of the question and make his own decision wisely, not handicapped by my neurotic anxiety.

A few years later he changed jobs again and I had to suffer a certain amount of anxiety once more, but I did not need to go through a week of depression first.

I could make the intellectual guess that anxiety about change derived from my loss of a home when my parents separated and I was boarded out with strangers in childhood. That thought, by itself, was no help; but I kept it on hand as helpful material, hoping some day I could make use of it in self therapy.

Then came a day when we had to start looking around for a new house. Every time Bernie suggested house hunting I developed a headache. About that time I began to get an occasional nervous tic, a twitch in my eyelid. One day I was thinking about moving and I felt like crying. My eyelid began to twitch. I grabbed pencil and paper and this is what I wrote:

"Feel like crying. Eye twitching. Why? Afraid to move? Give up this house I fell in love with at first sight? Lose something I love? Will never live in a house I love again. This was temporary.

like my childhood? The way I felt when I left New York? [At that time I was convinced I would never feel at home in Calif., never make new friends.] Can't imagine being at home & safe ever again. Going into alien house. Someone else's house like outsider. Have to pretend. Be a good sport. Like foster child. I don't want to be a foster child. Want to stay in my own home where I belong forever. Turn back the clock."

The child within me cried bitterly for a little while; then I felt better. The twitch in my eyelid disappeared and never came back. I was able to go househunting without headaches.

In the next few months I used self therapy twice to track down different aspects of my anxiety about moving: once thinking it through alone and once talking it out with a friend. Twice the child within me felt lost and displaced. By the time we had unpacked in the new house I was ready to settle down and love it just as I had loved the old one.

One emotion can mask another, but until you have dared to let yourself feel that apparent emotion, you cannot get down to the one it is hiding. Self therapy is a process of using any clues that come along. You never know when you are continuing the work you began some time earlier.

I once had a student who was a physician. He knew how eagerly I explore every avenue to discover anything new in psychology, so he very kindly offered to let me use his name to take current periodicals, professional journals, out of the medical library attached to the hospital medical school. All I had to do was pick up what I wanted from the open shelves, bring them to the librarian's desk and sign this doctor's name, as if I were doing research for him. Well, I was delighted at this opportunity to gobble up all that new material hot off the griddle and had visions of running wild among those psychiatric journals. I could hardly wait.

And yet, strangely enough, I kept putting off that trip to the medical library. Every day I would wake in the morning and think, "Today I'll treat myself. I'll go and get those journals." But somehow there was always something else I had to do that day. At last I began to pay attention to this peculiar reluctance and so I deliberately got into the car and set out for the library.

About half-way there I began to notice a pain in my back, the kind of cramp that comes from tensing up a muscle. This is an old habit of mine. Usually all I can do is deliberately relax those muscles for a minute and then absentmindedly go back to the tension again. There have been times when I kept this up so long that I ended up flat on my back for a week, unable to sit up.

This time I approached the back ache in a different way. I told myself this tension was a clue: I was obviously trying to avoid some emotion. What was I afraid to feel? I examined my immediate situation. Here I was finally going to the medical library after all that delay. But why had I put it off so long? What was there about this set-up that troubled me? I tried to visualize myself walking into the medical library, looking around for the shelves where the psychiatric journals must be stacked. I would not know where they were; I might have to ask the librarian for help; or she would see me wandering around looking lost and ask me what I was doing there. The thought terrified me. Fear—that was what I had been trying not to feel. I let myself feel it now, a sharp physical pang deep in the viscera. The librarian would know at a glance that I was not a doctor, that I did not belong there, that I was, in fact, an imposter! This fear lasted only a few seconds but when it went away the tension in my back muscles went too. I drove to the library relaxed and comfortable, curious to watch myself in this new adventure and see what would happen now that I knew what my problem was. The fascinating thing about letting yourself feel fear is that you are now freer to act the way you want to and you have a new sense of adventure. For a while you transcend your weakness, but with a spontaneity and aliveness that is very different from the rigid control used to deaden yourself to your true feelings.

So I parked my car and walked to the library entrance carefully paying attention to whatever feeling might come along. As soon as I crossed the threshold that pang of fear gripped me again. But it went in a second and I was able to walk slowly, head straight ahead as if I knew where I was going, eyes avidly but inconspicuously scanning the walls on both sides as I went. In short order I came upon stacks of periodicals listed in alphabetical order and it was easy to find what I wanted.

How might I have acted if I had been hiding my fear from myself, rigidly in control? My usual method would be to scurry in, dash madly about, searching for those shelves and immediately draw attention to myself; or else (the hidden fear forcing me to act frightened against my will) timidly approach the librarian and helplessly beg for aid with such a worried look as to arouse her suspicions of my motives.

As it was, I rapidly collected ten journals, decided that would be too conspicuous, cut it down to five, and then slowly, with an expression of poise and calm, approached the librarian's checkout desk. And then once again the sharp pang of fear. I waited a second or two until it had waned, then laid the journals on her desk. My usual way would have been to wait fearfully for her to ask for my card or credentials, and then rush into anxious explanations of my status. Instead, the fear having already come and gone, I was able to say casually, before she asked anything, "These are for Dr. L."

She looked a little surprised and said, "Is Dr. L. on our hospital staff?"

For a moment the fear clawed its way out again and threatened to stifle me. (Was she going to throw me out?) But it was gone in an instant and I was able to raise my eyebrows, and say, "Of course." And that was all there was to it. She checked me out and all was well. I got out of there without anyone noticing me: no one pointed a finger and screamed, "J'accuse!"

There is a sequel to this story in the chapter on "Dependency."

HOW TO SAFELY FEEL A "DANGEROUS" EMOTION

NOTICE THE quotes around "dangerous" in the title. This means no emotion is really dangerous, but some of them feel that way to us. Up till now I have been talking about hidden feelings, but this chapter is about those feelings we deliberately swallow down. Psychologists call a hidden feeling "repressed." An emotion just near the surface, which you are *deliberately* trying not to feel is "suppressed." This chapter is about suppressed feelings.

Which feelings do we generally consider dangerous? Those we have learned are "bad": hate, anger, fear, anxiety, jealousy. But even a "good" feeling, like love, can sometimes be felt as dangerous. A woman who has been rejected by a man is sure she hates him now and may be ashamed to feel any last glimmer of love for him. She will push that feeling down because it feels dangerous: she thinks it may lead her to further suffering.

But we cannot afford to swallow any of our emotions down. No one can afford to decide in advance to feel certain kinds of feelings and not others. You are not a god: you did not make yourself. You were born with the capacity to feel whatever humans can feel. To discard whole areas of natural feelings is a dangerous game. If you stop feeling "bad" emotions, after a while you cannot feel many "good" one either. The person who is afraid to feel anger or hate becomes less capable eventually of loving. The more rigid you are, in the terrible effort to control your feelings, the less warm and spontaneous you will be; you lose the capacity for deep feelings of any kind.

Not everyone can practice self therapy without professional help; sometimes a psychotherapist is necessary before one can peel away the layer of the apparent feeling and feel the hidden emotion. But everyone can learn to *feel his apparent feelings*. You can improve your emotional health considerably if you dare to feel those surface feelings, whatever emotion comes along, instead of picking and choosing which seem safest.

Why do we avoid an emotion? 1. It is something your intellect warns you not to act out, like yelling at your boss, beating your child, forcing your loved one to reject you, making a fool of yourself. You have not yet learned to separate *feeling* from *action*. Long ago your mother said something like, "Don't be angry with your sister." She should have said, "Don't be mean to your sister." You have a right to feel anything at all, but you cannot always afford to express your feelings in direct action, not if you want to win friends and influence people. You may be afraid anger will force you into violent action, or fear make a coward of you, so you try to avoid these "dangerous" emotions. Unfortunately, the less aware you are of a feeling, the more power it has to force you into self-defeating action. The best way to gain control over your action is to feel this emotion as intensely as possible. Once you have felt it, you will be free to decide calmly how to act, how to avoid the behavior that may bring on shame, guilt, loss of self-respect.

One of my students was faced with new and frightening responsibility and she wanted desperately to rise to this challenge with courage and strength. Soon she began to notice a chronic mood of irritability: she was giving her family a hard time and hating herself. She took time out to talk about this symptom with a good listener. "What am I afraid to feel?" she asked herself. "What's new in my life? When did I begin to feel so cranky?" In a little while she found the answer: helplessness, fear, was what she had been swallowing down. Afraid to *feel* like a coward because she thought it would make her *act* like one. She let herself break down for a few minutes and cry like a scared child carrying the burden of an adult. It was painful experience but it did not last long. After that she was able to be the responsible adult she wanted to be. The crabbiness disappeared. Later it returned once in a while, but each time she was able to dispel it by giving herself permission to feel helpless for a few minutes; she found it easier to act like a brave person after she had faced her fear.

2. Another reason we try not to feel "bad" emotions is the fear that this means we *are* bad. Existential psychology emphasizes the concept of responsibility. You are responsible for your *actions,* not your thoughts. (Jewish tradition teaches that God made man in His own image: that is, with the knowledge of right and wrong and the ability to make choices; each time a man chooses wrong-doing it is easier for him to do wrong next time, and each time he does right it strengthens him to make the next right decision.) The Existential-

ists tell us that man has some control over his moral development. He is not merely a product of his past experiences: he is also what he is becoming. The more freely you can feel all your emotions, the greater is your ability to act the way you want to, to become the person you want to be. The point is, the bad person is one whose *actions* are bad. If your actions are good, you *are* good, no matter what "bad" thoughts and feelings you have.

3. Another thing that troubles us is the irrational fear that others can read our minds. Always tell the truth to your mother. Mother knows when her little girl is fibbing." Small children are not too clear about parents' mysterious powers. It takes a long time to learn that we have complete privacy inside our own heads. Some of us never do learn that: we still have a sneaking suspicion that no matter how sweetly we smile, the other fellow can see hatred in our eyes. That is nonsense. We are all better actors than we give ourselves credit for: nobody can read your mind. Have you never gazed at a lecturer's face with a rapt look and your mind far away? You seem to be hanging on every word; he has no way of knowing you are bored to tears. It is perfectly possible to feel anger, hate, fear, jealousy and not show it.

I used to develop splitting headaches every time I chatted with a certain neighbor. I finally figured out what was the matter. I could not stand her, and while I could face these bad thoughts when she was not around, I never allowed myself to feel dislike when I was with her. I acted as if she could read my mind: I had to keep back those thoughts and force myself to feel friendly while I talked with her.

I solved my problem in my own way. I knew I was not brave enough yet to think "bad" thoughts while facing her, so from then on I was careful to avoid conversations with this lady. Whenever I met her I smiled and hurried on, reminding myself that I couldn't stand her. No headaches.

4. The very small child believes thoughts have magic power. If a person he has hated sickens or dies the child suffers terrible guilt. Adults still harbor some of that superstition: we are afraid to think ill of someone for fear of the evil potency of our thoughts. This belief in magic is absurd. Face facts: when you do harm to a person you hurt him; but your thoughts have no such power. You can think anything at all as long as you use reason to guide your actions. Let's outgrow these delusions of grandeur; we're just not that powerful.

5. Sometimes you are afraid of the violence of an emotion. You cannot stop yourself feeling a little angry, let us say, but you dare not let yourself feel the full intensity of rage for fear it may overwhelm you. Your potential fury seems so powerful you imagine you will fall apart, disintegrate, if you let it out. Try it and see how wrong you were. Let yourself go; feel the emotion as intensely as you can. Try writing it out. One student found writing gave her permission to feel a dangerous emotion she had been choking back all her life. Perhaps you are afraid of an intense emotion because you do not know a safe way to channel it. Writing helps you feel it and also gives you something to do with the emotion. It relieves some of the frustration of having to control your actions (like kicking the other fellow in the teeth).

The first year I sailed, I noticed every time Bernie and I came back from an hour on the rough waters of the bay I was utterly exhausted. After many months I began to wonder about that fatigue and to watch myself. I observed that all the time we were out on the water I was desperately pressing both hands down with all my strength, as if, all by myself, I had to keep that eighteen foot sailboat from tipping over. I never let myself feel scared; instead I tensed up every nerve and muscle. No wonder I was exhausted when the ordeal was over.

What would happen if I let myself feel fear? Next time we went out I experimented. As soon as we were out on the bay, where the water was rough, I began to tighten up in that absurd attempt to control both myself and the boat. So I deliberately unwound, looked out at the waves and let the fear take over. Now for the first time fear washed over me and for a few seconds I could hardly breathe. But then it was gone and I felt comfortably relaxed. For the rest of that hour's sail I had the strange experience of that wave of fear every fifteen minutes or so, each time lasting less than a minute. For the rest of the time I found myself enjoying sailing as I had never done before. Instead of a sacrifice for Bernie's sake (the Absolutely Perfect Wife shares her husband's hobbies), it was a thrilling adventure, well worth the occasional pangs of fear.

6. One who has studied psychology or dabbled in psychotherapy without ever feeling his hidden feelings may come to think of himself as just another case history. He uses the latest psychiatric jargon and talks glibly of his Oedipus complex, but he intellectualizes about his unconscious motivation instead of feeling. When his intellect tells

him some apparent emotion is "merely" a neurotic defense he stops feeling it. The emotion is irrational so he thinks he does not have to feel it: he rises above it. This kind of person is so adept at "analyzing" other people that he refuses to react to them in a spontaneous way ("Poor neurotic, he's feeling hostile today; I mustn't take offense.")

I explained at the beginning of this chapter why you cannot afford to avoid irrational feelings. Besides, if you notice an inappropriate reaction, you must feel that apparent emotion if you hope to get through to the hidden feeling. Self therapy, any kind of psychotherapy or analysis, is impossible for one who will not let himself feel his surface emotions.

Suppose you swallow down an apparent feeling simply because you know it is a defense, a cover for a deeper feeling. You then have to develop another layer, a new defense to cover this one you dare not feel. For example, you choke down anger because your intellect suspects it is pseudo-anger, a cover for something else. If you do this regularly, you may find yourself feeling anxiety or headache or some other painful symptom as a cover for that anger: layer on layer. This is the way to become more neurotic, burdening yourself with more symptoms, narrowing down your scope of areas in which you can function comfortably. It also adds to the work of self therapy or professional psychotherapy when you finally get around to using one of the uncovering techniques.

What can we do with these "dangerous" emotions when reason warns us not to act them out? When in doubt, do nothing. Some people have a tendency to rush into impulsive action to avoid feeling. The soldier who dashes into danger blindly to get away from his fear exposes himself foolishly, disregarding common sense and learned strategy. The person who hates the anxiety of decision-making feels any decision is better than this internal conflict. Whenever you act just to avoid a painful feeling, your behavior is self-defeating, you make the wrong decisions. Not sure whether your child needs discipline or permissiveness at this moment? Feel helpless? Resist the temptation to act powerful. When in doubt do nothing; get away and think it over. Stop and let yourself feel. Talk it out, write it out, cry it out. When you have felt this "dangerous" emotion intensely, you will be freer to use your intellect for a wiser choice of action.

When you are trying not to feel, you distort what you see and hear: the problem is confusing. But after you let yourself feel whatever you need to, the whole situation becomes clearer; you can understand what is going on.

One evening, just as I was settling down with a good book, Bernie announced that he had to pick up his car at the mechanic's and I would have to go with him. I was tired, not in the mood for night driving. "Hmn . . . where is this mechanic?" I asked doubtfully.

"Downtown Palo Alto."

"Oh . . . well, do I have to go with you? Just take my car." Patiently, as to an idiot child, Bernie explained that sure he could drive there in my car, but it would be difficult to drive both cars back home. "Yeah, that's right." I giggled a little in embarrassment. "Where is this mechanic?"

"Downtown Palo Alto."

"Do you have to get it tonight? How about tomorrow?"

"I need it for work tomorrow morning. Unless you want to drive me in tomorrow and pick me up."

"Oh, no. OK I'll go with you tonight. Just give me a little while to rest up." So Bernie waited and by the time he wanted to leave I was feeling better and resigned to my fate.

He got behind the wheel: he would drive there and I would drive my car back. As I climbed in beside him, I asked anxiously, "Just where is this mechanic?"

For some odd reason, Bernie blew his top. "For God's sake," he yelled, "we're going there. You'll see when we get there. What's the matter with you?" His sudden anger took me by surprise. I felt like giggling, but it's not a good idea to laugh in an angry person's face, so I bit back my giggles. But the harder I tried to control it, the more hysterical I felt. Why was Bernie angry? Why did I feel so giggly? I remembered how the pre-adolescent giggles nervously when an adult scolds him. What was I afraid to feel?

Deliberately I unwound my tensed muscles and let myself go; I felt—fear! For a brief moment I felt like a helpless child, afraid of a threatening, angry adult: painful and humiliating for a woman my age with the kindest husband in the world. The fear lasted a few seconds and when it was gone, the nervous tendency to giggle was gone too. Now the whole picture made sense to me. No wonder Bernie was annoyed. That monotonous repetition, "Where is this mechanic?" meant, to his ears, that I was still dragging my feet, still unwilling to help him out this evening.

101

I had never confided my fear of night driving. The only way I feel safe after dark on the road is with a detailed map in my head. Since I knew now what was bothering him, I told Bernie why I was so anxious for directions. His anger melted away. "What are you worried about?" he reassured me. "You'll follow my car home."

This did not satisfy me. "No, I might lose your car. I have to know exactly how to get home." So Bernie gave explicit directions about each street and turning and described where the mechanic was downtown. All's well that ends well.

Moral: No matter how foolish your apparent feeling is, feel it. In fact, the sillier it is, the more necessary it is to feel it before you can plan any intelligent action. When you are afraid to feel, you have trouble understanding what the other fellow is feeling: he is a mystery to you.

SHAME AND GUILT

WE TEND to lump shame and guilt together without differentiating between them. Classical psychoanalysis has been mainly concerned with guilt: guilt about sex was the most common source of neurosis among Freud's patients. There has been until recently little study of shame discussed in the psychiatric literature. How does guilt differ from shame? You suffer guilt when you have transgressed your moral code. Guilt is something for which you hope to atone. Shame, on the other hand, has little to do with morals; it is more a matter of taste. And you cannot atone for shame.

You feel shame when you think you have made a fool of yourself: you feel exposed before a mocking audience and you wish the earth would open up and swallow you. You come to a party horribly over-dressed or you dream you are walking down Main Street naked. Oddly enough, you can feel shame when no one else notices your *faux pas;* even when you are alone. An excellent, scholarly book on this is *On Shame and the Sense of Identity* by Helen Lynd.

Some cultures are guilt oriented, like Freud's nineteenth century Austria. Denmark is a culture where guilt is the chief disciplinary measure in child-rearing. Hendin, in *Suicide and Scandinavia,* reports an interview he had with a Danish patient that, he says, is typical of this background. She was beginning to tell him about her unhappy childhood, then refused to go on talking. When he asked why, she told him, "You probably had a happy childhood and it will make you feel too guilty to hear about mine."

When the small Danish child is naughty, instead of punishing him his mother says, "You are breaking your mother's heart." Suicide, according to this study, commonly has the meaning, "When you discover how unhappy I am, you'll feel guilty."

Japan is a country where people are strongly motivated by shame, the need to "save face." For a vivid picture of this read Ruth Benedict's beautiful anthropological study, *The Sword and the Chrysanthemum.*

American Indians are shocked at our use of physical punishment for children. They have always shamed their children into socially accepted behavior. For a psychoanalytic discussion of this, read *Childhood and Society* by Erik Erikson. Recent tourist reports on nursery schools in the Soviet Union seem to indicate a similar trend.

This country used to be more guilt-oriented than it is now. Those were the days of rugged individualism. Today, with the emphasis on winning friends and influencing people, the craving for popularity and keeping up with the Joneses, the fear of sticking our necks out, being different, we seem to be more and more influenced by shame. For a sociologist's interpretation read David Reisman's *The Lonely Crowd* and *Individualism Reconsidered*. We suffer both shame and guilt.

Why all this sociology and anthropology? In self therapy, it helps to have a sense of proportion. When you can see what your background, your culture, has done to you, you can observe yourself more clearly. Self-awareness is the first step toward finding hidden feelings.

PART I: SHAME

You can only be ashamed of someone you love. If you did not care about him, his behavior might disgust or anger you, but you would not feel shame. In our culture, where family groups are close-knit and children are so dependent on their parents, one of the tasks of adolescence is to free oneself from this dependency. The adolescent, in his need to find his own identity and to be ready to fall in love with a stranger, falls out of love with his parents. This is when he is ashamed of them: everything they do seems to embarrass him. Both the young person and his parents should remember that if he did not love them, he would not feel shame. This knowledge can spare him guilt about his shame and the adults can survive this painful period with some humor.

Self therapy can help you cope with shame. One of my students is a writer. She met an editor at a party and later decided to invite her to lunch, hoping to strengthen this social contact and gain professionally.

She worked hard polishing up her house, prepared elegant and exotic dishes, and was tense and exhausted when her guest arrived. "From then on," she told me later, "everything went wrong!" The menu was too unusual for the editor's taste, the hostess too ill-at-ease and tired for witty conversation. She was relieved when her guest left early, and went to her room to lie down and rest after her ordeal. But she could not relax. She thought how little she had accomplished with that lunch; it was a wasted day. 'Round and 'round her thoughts went, like a broken record: why had she done this, why hadn't she done that, if only she had said something-or-other instead of. . . . Obsessive, boring, maddening.

As she tossed and turned in frustration, it dawned on her that obsessive thinking is always a clue to something hidden. Step by step she began to track down the hidden feeling with self therapy. In a little while she had it: shame. She was ashamed of wasting her day, ashamed because she had known from the start that this editor had not been interested in her work, ashamed because she felt she had made a fool of herself.

What can you do with shame? You cannot atone for it; you cannot appease your conscience with self punishment. All you can do is face it: feel it. Sweat it out courageously until it leaves you. This student, when she uncovered the shame, let herself feel it for a few painful minutes. Then it was gone and the obsessive thinking was gone too.

We all have to feel shame at times. The trouble is, we go to great lengths to avoid it, cover it up. Remember that the apparent emotion, the pseudo-feeling, lasts much longer than the true feeling once it comes out. If you dare to feel shame, you can avoid doing that foolish thing again; but if you do not allow yourself to know you are ashamed, you cannot learn from experience and you will get yourself in this awkward spot again.

One day I read an article in the *Saturday Review* about the Polish Ladies. The Nazis had performed "experimental" operations on these women "in the interest of science." The account of these maimed survivors and the horrors they had suffered made me physically ill. I began to tremble and felt nauseated, had trouble breathing, my heartbeats were irregular. I felt weak and lay down. Finally I was able to shed a few weak tears and those physical symptoms disappeared. But I could not forget that story. All day I cried quietly as I went about my housework, and when Bernie came home I found I could not bear to tell him about it: I had to keep it a secret. This fact, plus obsessive thinking, pointed to the need for self therapy: they were inappropriate reactions, Step 1.

Step 2. Feel the apparent emotion. I felt helpless despair. What could I do about the Polish Ladies? Step 3. What else did I feel? I remembered those physical symptoms, the nausea, trembling, etc. These all added up to anxiety.

Step 4. What did this remind me of? The automatic horror and fear with which I always reacted to any thought of Nazis. In my mind's eye, a Nazi was a stereotype: ruthless, brutal, cold, *inhuman*, a kind of robot. What else did this remind me of? My mixed feelings about the German language which sounds so like Yiddish, the language of my grandparents, the language I spoke as a small child. It was always strangely disturbing to hear the similarity between Yiddish and German, to remember that Yiddish is based on German. To hear a movie-Nazi speak in a language I could partly understand, because I once spoke Yiddish, shook me up. Why? Because we had something in common, those inhuman robots and I? Suddenly the thought slipped out: all men are brothers; Nazis are not robots, they are human like me. And then I felt a new emotion, the hidden one— shame. I was ashamed to belong to the human race when humans could do what these had done. My brothers!

After a while I was able to talk to Bernie about it and talking helped a little. It must have been the hidden shame that kept me silent before. Then, I could think of something to do to relieve the helpless despair. I wrote a letter to the magazine editor expressing my feelings and enclosing a check to be used toward a program of rehabilitation for the Polish Ladies. Once you feel your true feelings you find you can act, you can do something to ease that feeling of helplessness. My obsessive thinking was gone.

PART II: GUILT

There are three kinds of guilt: neurotic, existential and real. Each of them may be hidden by apparent feelings, each can be uncovered with professional or self therapy, but there is a basic difference. You need only *feel* neurotic guilt in order to get rid of the symptom (the apparent emotion), but feeling is not enough with existential and with real guilt. With them, you have to *do* something about the problem in real life.

Remember how I forgot Bernie's lunch ("Thinking it Through, Alone")? I used anger to cover the hidden guilt about "depriving" him of food. He did not feel deprived at all: my hidden guilt was irrational, neurotic. All I had to do was feel that guilt and the apparent anger disappeared; I had no trouble with that problem afterward. I have to use self therapy to feel that guilt from time to time. Remember my pseudo-anger when Jeanie nagged me about meals? ("Communication Between Parent and Child" Part II.) There is nothing else to do with neurotic guilt but feel it.

Real guilt may be hidden by an apparent emotion or neurotic symptom (headache) just like neurotic guilt. It too can be uncovered by the same techniques. But when you have felt that hidden real guilt, it is not enough to recognize it and accept it; you then have to find some way to atone for what you have done, or left undone, before you get rid of the symptom. Formerly, this kind of problem was handled by the clergyman who gave guidance. Traditionally the classical psychoanalyst has been concerned only with neurotic guilt. Today very few people turn to religion for help in this area. The Existential psychologists point out that the psychotherapist can no longer limit his responsibility to the problem of   guilt. For further discussion on this, read Victor Frankl's book, *From Death Camp to Existentialism* and *The Doctor and the Soul*.

I read an article in *The Nation* about the Reverend Ashton Jones. This white, Methodist minister, born and bred in the Deep South, has spent the greater part of his life traveling around preaching the brotherhood of man. He was the first freedom-rider, the first to use sit-ins. The article told how this man is being crucified for daring to live his religion, described in dreadful detail the brutality of the Southern police, the injustice of the courts, the awesome courage and faith of Ashton Jones. I began to cry as I read it, and I cried off and on all day. At last I recognized that my obsessive thinking was an inappropriate reaction, Step 1. The apparent feeling, Step 2., was grief and helplessness. Step 3. What else did I feel? Rage at man's inhumanity to man, and something else. . . .

Step 4. What did this remind me of? Ashton Jones was being crucified for acting out his religion. He was trying to imitate Jesus, taking the whole burden of mankind's injustice on his own frail shoulders. I was angry. Why? Angry at a world that forces one man to do so much all by himself? Angry with Ashton Jones for daring to assume that burden. That was the rest of Step 3 (What else did I feel?). It had taken me a while to put my finger on it.

What did that make me think of? My religion, Judaism, teaches a very different message from Christianity: each man must seek his own salvation; no one can atone for another's sins. When the Children of Israel aroused God's anger, Moses offered to take their punishment on himself. But God said no man can assume responsibility for another, atone for another. I am not a religious person, but evidently this concept was deeply ingrained in me, because I suddenly realized I was horrified to think Ashton Jones was trying to assume *my* responsibility. That was my hidden feeling: guilt; it overwhelmed me for a painful minute. I, who believe all men are brothers; I who feel so deeply about segregation; what was I doing about it? Sitting safely up here in the North, mouthing platitudes to other Liberals, shelling out a few dollars to organizations who promised to fight the good fight for me, passing the buck to Ashton Jones who was living out my ideals.

Step 5. Look for the pattern. I had noticed long ago that whenever I thought or read about the problems of deprived minority groups I was overcome with anxiety symptoms. I had explained it to myself: I was over-identifying with them, being a member of a minority group myself. But now I realized this was only a part of the explanation; that often my anxiety was a cover for guilt: I was doing so little in a cause that meant so much to me.

This was real guilt, not neurotic. I could not rest until I had done something. Finally I wrote a letter to Ashton Jones telling him just how I felt, and enclosing the first in a series of checks to help him from time to time with lawyers' fees, bail, etc. This started a wonderful correspondence and gave me a chance to get a little more involved, if only on the safe, cowardly basis of money. I am not a brave person. But later that year I found an opportunity to work on a local problem, which I would formerly have avoided out of anxiety, and get really involved in a situation which was painful for me but brought genuine results. For the first time I was able to assume responsibility and a measure of leadership in a frightening situation, and follow it through to a successful conclusion. My new-found courage was based on knowledge of my hidden guilt. Each time you do something real to lighten the burden of your real guilt, you suffer less from the symptom, the apparent emotion. I had to go through self therapy again a few years later and feel that hidden, real guilt again, but it was easier than the first time. After that I found I could read material on these painful subjects (newspapers etc.) without my old anxiety symptoms and headaches. I am freer to think about such problems; but more important, I am freer to act.

Existential guilt is something you suffer when you fail to fulfill your true potential. If you have some artistic gift, some creative ability which you are not using, you pay the penalty of existential guilt, which may be covered up by some apparent emotion, or physical symptom, just like neurotic guilt. But when you discover the existential guilt you must do something about it, as with real guilt, before you can get rid of the symptom. It is not enough to feel it, as with neurotic guilt.

One of the common symptoms of existential guilt is the insatiable desire for passive recreation. Whether you are doping yourself up with television or more highbrow pursuits like opera, ballet or theatre, does not really matter. That starved feeling, that craving to be entertained, is a clue that you should be doing something creative. This is a cover that may be misleading to others; only you, yourself can recognize it. For instance, reading appears to be a praise-worthy activity, especially to non-readers. But to a compulsive reader like me, the yearning to drown myself in books is a bad sign: there is something else I should be doing (probably writing) but I do not want to think about it. Sometimes I get an overwhelming urge to go out and do something festive: see a movie, dine in a plush restaurant, *spend money*. This frequently happens on a Saturday night, and if Bernie is tired or there are no good movies in town, I begin to feel like a caged lion: restless, dissatisfied, angry. I discovered, by accident, that if I sit down and play the piano for a long time I end up feeling relaxed and satisfied, perfectly happy to spend a quiet evening at home. The craving to go out was a cover for an inner need to do something creative.

Self therapy has taught me that I must write; otherwise I suffer existential guilt. I do not enjoy writing; I prefer to lecture. But I find that when I stick to my daily stint at the typewriter, I can manage also to stick to my diet. I have less trouble with my compulsive eating. I have traced other symptoms to existential guilt too: tension, boredom and mild depression. Whenever I go back to writing, these disappear.

Suppose you have some talent unknown to yourself, simply because you have never been exposed to that activity? How can you avoid existential guilt in these areas? The answer is in the chapter, "How to Free Your Natural Creativity": experiment with activities for which you have no talent, or think you have no talent, and see what happens.

THE HIDDEN CRAVING FOR DEPENDENCY

IF YOU are hiding within you a child who still feels deprived, still craves the kind of love a mother gives the helpless infant, it is important to let that child come out into the open. If you keep that desire hidden from yourself, you may have one of two typical self-defeating patterns: 1) you may act out that craving without being aware of it, or 2) you may do just the opposite; pretend to yourself that you are completely independent. Either extreme is dangerous.

1) There is the woman who expects her friend to devote more time, care and attention to her than is reasonable, is insatiable in her irrational demands, and eventually, inevitably, makes a pest of herself. The friend is finally forced to reject her. This poor lady is unaware that the child within her expects the friend to be her loving mother. She does not notice her own self-defeating behavior and cannot figure out what happened. The tragedy is that every time she loses a friend (and this keeps on happening) the child within her suffers: the hidden craving for dependency grows more intense.

2) Then there is the opposite type, the man who goes through life proving to himself and others how strong and independent he is. He tends to develop peptic ulcer symptoms when his first child is born. The child within him feels neglected when his wife's attention is bound up with the baby. But the knowledge that he wants to be babied, that there is a child within him, is so damaging to his self-esteem (built on his inner picture of the strong, self-reliant male) that he keeps it hidden. It is the conflict between these two inner needs, the craving for dependency versus the idealized self-image of independence, which causes the ulcer symptom. This can develop into a full-fledged ulcer unless he can peel away a layer and feel his true feeling, the hidden dependency.

In our culture, the adolescent faces the developmental task of growing away from his parents, developing his own identity. He still has one foot in childhood: an urge to keep on doing the safe thing, be Mother's good boy, hold on to the security of those early years. But he senses that this is a dangerous tendency, that he must move

110

forward toward maturity, so there is a steady battle within him between his need to become independent and the old craving for dependency. Often when he seems to hate his parents ("You're keeping me tied to your apron-strings. Let me live my own life! You never want me to have any fun.") It is really his own dependency craving he hates. But he cannot afford to recognize this self-hatred: it is easier to project it on to adults.

I once heard Fritz Redl lecture. (Author of *Children Who Hate* and *Controls From Within*.) He said we have done a good job freeing our children from dependency on authority figures. This new generation is not awed by teachers, etc., and would not easily be led by a Führer. Unfortunately we have done too good a job, he said, selling them the importance of winning friends and being popular. They are so desperately dependent on the approval of their peers that we now have a brand new problem. A gang of boys with an antisocial leader has always had some kids on the fringes who themselves have no real destructive tendencies. Until recently, these would drift away from the group when the activity became frankly delinquent. Today we have a new phenomenon, something Redl calls a low threshold of contamination: these basically non-hostile, border-line youngsters are caught up in the mood of the gang and go along with the others rather than be called "chicken." In my chapter, "Shame and Guilt," I mentioned David Reisman's analysis of the modern American who is becoming dependent on the approval of others, to the point of giving up his true identity as an individual.

I mentioned too, the study on Denmark which was begun to investigate the high suicide rate in that country. They found that Danes are encouraged to be dependent. The small child is not given the kind of approval for new achievements as in our culture. Instead, he is made to feel he is a good boy when he sticks close to Mother and does not strike out on his own. Young people largely enter marriage either to be dependent on someone, or (identifying with Mother) to encourage the other to lean on him.

Helena Deutch, in *The Psychology of Women*, says that to the extent to which a woman has not resolved her dependency on her own mother, she will have difficulty with her own daughter, especially during adolescence. By "resolving her dependency" she means chiefly feeling her hidden dependency craving, coming to terms with it. We can broaden her statement to include fathers and sons too. The adult who cannot face his own hidden dependency needs will not be able to

111

accept his child's struggles in this area, will confuse the roles of adult and child. In general, the less aware you are of the child within you, the less capable you are of acting like an adult.

In the chapter, "Anxiety and Fear," I discussed Karen Horney's theory about the basic conflict between dependency and hostility. Also Rollo May's concept of the struggle against dependency involved in every creative act.

About twelve years ago I began to notice a peculiar symptom. Every two hours I would develop a stomach ache which could be relieved by certain foods, preferably milk. Raw fruit or salad made it worse. We had been living in the Midwest for a year and a half where Bernie was back at college, under the G.I. Bill. Now we were home in New York, he had a job and everything was fine. For the first time I started to pay attention to these two-hour pains. When I mentioned them to Bernie he wanted to know how long this had been going on. I thought for a while and then said, about a year. "A year! You never said anything about it. Why didn't you tell me before?" I did not know. I just had not thought about it. (Freud described "la belle indifférence" to physical pain shown by certain patients who use physical symptoms to hide emotional pain.) Bernie said it sounded like an ulcer. Of course! Why had I never thought of that? Obviously a peptic ulcer. Funny I never realized it.

He dragged me to a doctor who promptly diagnosed peptic ulcer symptom and prescribed a bland diet as the first step. Diffidently I asked if ulcers weren't usually due to psychological factors. "Yes, yes, tension. Relax!" he barked as he hurried me out to make room for the next item on his assembly line. All the way home I tried desperately to relax. But when it came to the bland diet I balked. For one thing, it was too fattening. Besides, my pride was outraged. How could I, who knew so much about psychology, have anything so embarrassing as a psychosomatic illness? I had to get rid of it fast. If there were low-cost psychiatric clinics then I had never heard of them, so I had to use self therapy. I recognized the ulcer symptom as Step 1, an inappropriate reaction.

Step 2. Feel apparent emotion. I began to think out loud while Bernie listened. In order to track down the apparent feeling, I needed to trace the symptom to its origin. When did I first begin having these two-hour pains? A year ago. That was when we left the Midwest to visit New York during a break between terms. What happened during that week's visit? I had a good time with old friends; saw both my parents . . . had some trouble. Dad had been quarreling with me, laying down the law, trying to make decisions for me that he had no right to make. Every time I left him, I cried. "He used to be such a loving father when I was little," I used to tell Bernie, "and now he looks at me with hatred in his eyes. I can't stand it! And I can't stand the way he talks to me."

Bernie wanted to know why I put up with it. "You're a big girl now. What's the matter with you?" So with his moral support, I rehearsed a brave speech and next day I told Dad off. I warned him that he would have to treat me more respectfully, that things had changed and I was no longer the deprived, love-starved child, that he'd better face the fact that he needed me more than I needed him now; if he continued to make me so miserable I would just stop visiting him. Poor Dad was shaken to see the worm turn, and he was charming and courteous for the rest of that week.

Bernie and I were both so proud of me that I got cocky and began sticking pins in my mother. She and I, the following day were involved in one of the pseudo-intellectual discussions that characterized our relationship at that time, when I did a cruel thing, unthinkingly. Under the guise of sincerity I interpreted for her: I told her the unconscious meaning (according to the books) of one of her patterns, in glib imitation of the stuff I was reading then. She brushed it off and we parted on friendly terms. But a week later, back at college, I realized what I had done and I was sorry. I wrote a letter of apology, embarrassingly "sincere," and Mother sent back a scorching reply, berating me for my cruelty and coldness, calling me an "unnatural" daughter. I wrote back defending myself hotly, reminding her of painful memories we had both politely ignored for decades. I blamed her for my neurotic tendencies and then ended with an impassioned plea for a new and honest relationship as two adults. I was trying to understand her, I said, in order to understand myself. She stopped writing.

What did I feel then, a year ago, during that correspondence and immediately after, when she did not reply? I remembered crying a great deal. Tears of rage, they seemed to be: I was so angry with Mother. "Who needs her?" I kept saying. "I'm grown up; I have my own family now!" Talking about it now to Bernie I began to feel angry all over again. That was Step 2. Feel the apparent emotion.

Step 3. What else did I feel? Just before I became so angry, when I first realized she was not going to write any more, I felt terrible grief and disappointment because my attempt at an honest relationship had failed.

Step 4. What does this remind me of? At first I could not think of anything helpful. Then I asked myself, what did I know about ulcer types. Maybe I could make use of all those case histories I had read. The ulcer type is usually an ambitious, aggressive man who cannot face his unconscious dependency cravings. "Well," I said despondently, "that's no help. I'm not a man, I'm not ambitious or aggressive (how little I knew myself in those days), and I have always faced my dependency on you." I always have trouble sleeping when Bernie goes out of town. "Could I be hiding some other kind of dependency? *What did I seem to be doing?* I felt I had outgrown my need for my parents and I had told them so. Then this ulcer symptom came along. What about all that crying when my mother stopped writing? And I was so upset when Dad was angry with me. "Was it possible," I began tentatively, "that I was crying because . . . no, that's ridiculous. It sounds so silly, but *maybe* I was crying for something else. Not simply anger. Was I feeling like the five-year-old I once was when my parents left me and boarded me out with strangers?" I began asking these questions out of scientific curiosity, laughing at the absurd idea. But before I was finished talking, I was sobbing. The adult in me still protested, "This is nonsense. I'm grown-up now." But the child within me was reliving that early period, crying pitifully for lost, loved parents.

This process of finding the hidden feeling took longer to happen than to write about. When I finally dried my tears and glanced at the clock, four hours had gone by. For the first time in a year, I had lived through four hours without a stomach-ache. That was twelve years ago and it has never come back.

I dared to feel my hidden dependency, dared to let the child within me cry for her parents; that deprived child no longer needed to demand that two-hour feeding schedule. What about my infantile dependency on my parents? Will the child within me ever grow up? I do not know. I am not my own psychoanalyst. Remember the hidden feeling in "Swan Lake" in the chapter, "Sneaking up on the Hidden Feeling," and my experience with the teacher in "The Child Within the Adult?" I may have to live with this child all my life. All I can do is let her out from time to time, and get rid of as many cover symptoms as possible. I can act like a rational, self-reliant adult despite the irrational infantile craving inside.

In the chapter on "Anxiety and Fear" I told the story of my fear of the medical library. I was afraid to take material out of it, under a doctor's name (a student who wanted to help me) for fear of being seized as an imposter. Here is the sequel to that story.

I went to that library several times but after the first experience I no longer had to suffer fear or tension. Still, when I was at home thinking about the whole thing, I was uncomfortable. Did the librarian think I was doing research for Dr. L.? Of course, I told myself, as my student, Dr. L. will profit from anything I can learn from these psychiatric journals. And yet I was not happy; I knew I was going there under false pretenses. So I inquired about the cost of a library card for outsiders and found it was twenty-five dollars per year. Twenty-five dollars! I was appalled. I couldn't spend that much money just for a library card. I chewed this over for a few days, still faced with my reluctance to use Dr. L.'s name. Finally I talked to Bernie. He understood just how I felt about going under false pretenses. "Go ahead and get that card," was his advice.

"But twenty-five dollars!" I kept saying. "Such a lot of money for just one year. How can I spend that just for my own amusement?" Bernie pointed out that these were technical books, not novels; that I had a right to certain professional expenses. After all, he bought technical books on engineering and subscribed to professional magazines.

"At the rate you read, you'll get your twenty-five dollars' worth by the end of the year." It sounded logical and I was grateful for his permission to buy that card, but I could not seem to give myself permission. I dithered back and forth for days, unable to make a decision. Should I go on being an imposter and try to forget my squeamishness, or should I indulge in the terrible extravagance of twenty-five dollars?

At long last it occurred to me that this inability to make a decision, plus the obsessive thinking, indicated I might be hiding something from myself. (Step 1. Recognize an inappropriate reaction.) So I called up a friend who is a librarian and told her how I felt. She heard me out and then she laughed. "What's your problem?" she wanted to know. "If you can't stand using Dr. L's name, get yourself a card."

"You don't think it would be extravagant? I'd be the only one in the family using that card. Twenty-five dollars for just one year!"

"It won't break you. What's the matter with you? I've never known you to make such a fuss about money."

I began to explore my feelings. (Step 2. Feel the apparent emotion.) What was bothering me? I felt I was not entitled to spend that much money on books: I felt guilty about such extravagance. Step 3. What else did I feel before this guilt? When I first discovered the price of the card I was shocked and surprised. Why? Bernie wasn't surprised. My first reaction was, "They can't expect me to pay that much!"

Step 4. What does this remind me of? Guilt about spending money on books. . . . I don't worry much about other kinds of expenses. What do books mean to me? I'm a compulsive reader. In my unhappy childhood I drowned myself in books. . . . My foster mother took away my library card to punish me. I can still get emotional about that: two years starved of books when I needed them most. I seem to be trying to make up for those two years: greedy in libraries and book stores, panicky when I run out of reading material.

Libraries. How do I feel about libraries? Wherever I have lived, the local library has been my home away from home. I love to browse through the stacks until they become as familiar to me as the furniture in my home. I am usually the librarian's best customer. How do I feel about the librarian? She is always an important figure in my life. If she happens to be a cross old lady looking severely down her glasses at me, I carefully woo her until I can bask in an occasional wintery smile. Most librarians have liked me; they like to recommend the latest good book.

How do I feel about the librarian at the medical library? A little in awe of her, yet drawn to her and eager to win her approval.

And now the hidden feeling came out in a great rush: disappointment; the terrible disappointment of the rejected child. I wanted this librarian to like me, to love me, to open her precious stock to me. I was an outsider, not a doctor, as once I had been the foster child. I wanted this foster mother to love me more than her own children. I did not want to pay for library privileges: I wanted them to be given as a gift in loving-kindness. The child within me craved special recognition: love me because I am different.

Step 5. Look for the pattern. I saw now that I had been trying to undo the past: wipe out, by some kind of magic, the unloved years, the years of rejection. That was why I had been so reluctant to spend the twenty-five dollars; it had nothing to do with economy. The guilt about spending was a cover for the childish disappointment. I had felt that hidden feeling and now the maddening indecision was gone. I was still uncomfortable about using Dr. L's name and I had no way of knowing whether that discomfort was irrational or not (I am not my own psychotherapist); I only knew it felt right and natural finally to spend twenty-five dollars for a library card, and I did. My inhibitions about visiting the medical library disappeared and during that year I got more than my twenty-five dollars worth. By the following year I was satisfied to read current journals which I was free to do without a card, so long as I read them in the library. I am a rapid reader so there was no problem.

How did I feel toward the librarian after I had felt that hidden feeling about her? I lost my awe of her and found her a warm, helpful person. I discovered she knew who I was, had heard me lecture, and was interested in my work. This was the kind of acceptance the child within me craved and I found myself glowing with pleasure every time she spoke to me. But I am aware of my hidden tendency to treat her like a foster mother, to demand favoritism, so I keep careful watch of myself. My adult self can stay in control now that it has accepted the child within: I can avoid demanding too much attention; I can "transcend my neurosis."

THE MEANING OF SELF-ACCEPTANCE

KAREN HORNEY and Eric Fromn are psychoanalysts who have written helpful books for the layman, but I have a bone to pick with them. They describe self-acceptance as self-love. "You must learn to love yourself before you can love anyone else," they tell us. This is a pretty tough assignment for one who is beginning to look within himself and discover all kinds of unpleasant truths about himself. It may scare him off the whole, painful business of peeling away layers, feeling new and nastier feelings.

Seventeen years of self therapy have helped me evolve a different definition of self-acceptance. Self-acceptance means getting to know yourself, becoming more self-aware, and daring to feel anything that comes along. It means recognizing the absurdity of your over-simplified, idealized self-images and accepting the complexity of your many-layered personality with all its contradictions. It means letting yourself feel the archaic, hidden feeling even while you are embarrassed because it does not fit in with your adult self. Self-acceptance means resigning yourself to the fact that there is a child within that still feels as a child, learning new ways of acting in order to humor that child along, ceasing to torment it. Remember how I forgot Bernie's lunch ("Thinking it Through Alone")? The child within me suffered guilt, even though Bernie did not miss that sandwich. I am resigned to my irrational feelings about food: I know I cannot afford to deprive my family of meals.

Of course, the person who practices self therapy (or any kind of psychotherapy) hopes that some of those hidden, irrational feelings will disappear after a while, that more and more of the childish aspects of his character will grow up and give up their foolish, humiliating demands. But he cannot predict how much of this will happen, nor how soon. The wisest approach is to accept each new aspect of yourself as you discover it. You do not have to like it; you simply have to resign yourself to its existence. You can hope it will change, but do not count on that. Assume, for the time being, that it will not change, that this aspect of the child within you will continue to make

118

its fantastic demands. Then use this knowledge, this new awareness of your pattern, to change your behavior and avoid tormenting that inner child. Remember, I learned that the child within me wanted special approval from a father figure ("The Child Within Each Adult"). It was a long time before that child began to relax its demands a little. I spared it unnecessary suffering by remembering my pattern. I avoided being trapped over and over again into situations where I had to force a father figure to reject me. I spared that child further deprivation and humiliation.

When you feel a hidden emotion which is obviously foolish and embarrassing, do not tell yourself, "I must never feel this way again." Instead, remind yourself that you will probably be tempted to feel this hidden emotion again and to cover it up with the same old pseudo-emotion, the apparent feeling, which may trick you into self-defeating behavior once more. Recognizing this pattern, and learning to guard against it in the future, is the true meaning of self-acceptance. You accept the hidden feeling and avoid acting out the pattern by remembering it, avoiding the old stereotyped cover and compulsive behavior. You try a new kind of action based on your knowledge and experience, despite the irrational desires of the child within you.

Self-acceptance also includes paying attention to your body's language. What physical symptoms do you generally get when you are afraid to feel a "dangerous" or forbidden emotion? Learn to notice these symptoms and respect them instead of doping them up or ignoring them.

I kept a record of headaches for several months during a period when they were frequent. (This record-keeping was a step forward, in itself, as formerly I had always ignored headaches until they became violent.) The very first moment I noticed each headache, I jotted down the date and exact time. Then I tried to remember what happened earlier that day; which incident might have triggered it off; what emotion I might have been avoiding. After a while I saw a certain consistency in my headache pattern. In every case I had been faced with opposite feelings, one of which would have cancelled out the other if I dared to feel it. Example: I was out for a good time and something frustrating occurred, but I could not bear to feel frustrated as it would spoil my happy mood. Or: I felt loving and warm toward someone and that person did something which might make me hate him for a moment if I paid attention to it. So I swallowed down the rage to avoid spoiling the loving mood; etc.

119

One outcome of this record-keeping was my new ability to notice a headache right away, instead of ignoring it in the vain hope that it would go away. The great advantage in noticing the first twinge is the ability to ask yourself, "What am I afraid to feel?" Often you will dare to feel the "dangerous" emotion and avoid the full-blown headache.

But if you are like me you may have to face this fact: you are a person who sometimes chooses (unconsciously) a headache instead of a painful emotion. To know this, is part of self-acceptance. But if you are avoiding an emotion or a thought and are feeling physical pain instead, you cannot afford to ignore the pain. Instead, practice self-acceptance of the body's language: let yourself feel the headache. (For a detailed account of this approach read *Gestalt Therapy* by Perls.) Your headache is not something that just came to you out of the blue. You, yourself, are making your head hurt; you are squeezing the muscles in your head in order to avoid some emotion. Pay attention to what is going on. If you concentrate on the pain in its earliest stages, you may be able to answer the question, "What am I afraid to feel? What am I covering up with this headache?" This is the way I get rid of many headaches before they become too intense.

But I have noticed that even when I cannot answer that question, cannot feel the "dangerous" or forbidden emotion, I frequently lose that headache just by letting myself feel the physical pain, concentrating on it.

Remember, when you use self therapy and uncover a hidden feeling it may be painful but it does not last long; whereas, if you cover it up, the fake feeling goes on and on. In the same way, I notice that a headache, if ignored, lasts a long time; but if you concentrate on it right from the beginning, if you are willing to pay the price of physical pain in avoiding emotion, the headache does not last long.

Self-acceptance means the courage to suffer.

120

THE HIDDEN BELIEF IN MAGIC

PRIMITIVE MAN believes in magic, and so does the small child in our civilized world. The child within you still harbors that old belief and you need to bring those childish ideas out in the open once in a while. Like any hidden feeling, the faith in magic can trap you into self-defeating behavior. Once you are aware of it, your adult intellect can keep you from making a fool of yourself.

The person who looks at each new failure with the kind of fatalism that says, "Well, that's the kind of luck I always have; I'm fated to fail," generalizes about his life pattern instead of trying to examine this particular incident. He is saying, in effect, "Some powerful Being has put a magic spell on me. I am condemned to failure." This belief in magic is a way of avoiding responsibility for his own actions. He does not want to believe in cause and effect and he refuses to explore this immediate failure. Instead of asking himself, "What went wrong here? Did I handle things foolishly? Was I hiding something from myself?" he brushes the whole thing off. Instead of daring to feel the frustration and pain of this particular experience, he turns away from the apparent feeling and takes refuge in a vague self-pity: the Fates are against him. This self-defeating pattern can be broken if he realizes that the child within him still believes in magic. Once he recognizes his inappropriate reaction (he has been acting as if he, the adult, believed in magic) he can go on to explore the specific situation and begin to use his experience and intelligence to break out of his rut of failure.

I knew an intelligent woman who, despite her very real charm and rich cultural background, was lonely. She easily attracted people to her and then bored them to death whining about her troubles in a compulsive, monotonous way. Each time she lost a new friend she added this experience to what Edmund Bergler calls her "list of grievances"; it was to her just another proof that the gods were discriminating against her. This stereotyped picture of herself as a victim prevented her from using her intelligence and experience to help herself, spared her the important, painful question she should have asked herself, "What went wrong in this particular relationship?"

The hidden belief in magic can do odd things to us. For several years I was involved with a woman I never really liked, and I could not figure out how to break off our unpleasant connection. Marian and I were active in the same civic organization and had children the same age, but that was all we had in common. She was a hostile, angry person, suspicious of everyone around her and a vicious gossip who loved spreading false rumors about her innocent neighbors. All her basic values were the exact opposite to mine. Our conversations were really monologues by her with regularly interspersed "Uh-huh's" from me. There was no meeting of minds. In addition, Marian was a terrible bore. She used to phone me at least once daily and talk at me to the point of nausea. When I complained bitterly to Bernie he would look at me incredulously. "What's your problem?" he wanted to know. "What are you wasting your time for? Just get rid of her."

But I didn't have the heart to drop her. "She's so lonely, poor thing, a complete isolate. She needs me. She thinks I'm her friend." Bernie laughed sardonically but I felt trapped.

This uncomfortable relationship went on for several years. Then, one day, during a meeting of the organization to which Marian and I belonged, I said something in open meeting to which (unknown to me) she took offense: something she interpreted as a personal criticism of her. Next morning she phoned me and gave me a terrible tongue-lashing. I didn't know what hit me, and I fell all over myself protesting my innocence: "But . . . but I never meant anything like that. How could you think . . . but . . ." Marian was all wound up and I couldn't get a word in edgewise. I was miserable when she hung up. How could she suspect me of trying to hurt her? Didn't she know me better than that? Why would I deliberately hurt anyone? How terrible! Frantically I phoned others who had been present at that fatal meeting. "Marian says I hurt her feelings. Did you think I said anything so dreadful?"

Everyone agreed my statement had been harmless. "You know Marian," they laughed. Yes, I knew Marian and her tendency to look for trouble, her addiction to feuds, but this was the first time I myself was involved.

I could not put that phone talk out of my mind. All day I chewed over that same old cud and by the next day, having spent a restless night, I was no longer troubled by her poor hurt feelings: I found something new to worry about. Mulling over her angry words, I remembered a veiled threat about my position in the organization. She held an executive office; maybe she had the power to interfere with my work, stop me from doing what seemed very important to me at the time. This fear of Marian's power grew until it reached fantastic proportions and I could not rest. Finally I talked to Marian's superior, a branch officer, and told her the whole story. She knew Marian had a reputation for long-drawn-out feuds, and I asked about my own position and its security. No, she had no such powers and I wasn't to worry. "You know Marian!"

Next, my fear turned into anger. At last I was able to work up some righteous indignation. How dared she talk to me that way, as if I were a bad child or some inferior creature! Who did she think she was? The nerve; This shrill interior clamor continued without respite and I grew pretty tired of my thoughts. But it wasn't until the third day, driving alone in the car, that it occurred to me that this obsessive thinking was (Step 1.) an *inappropriate reaction.*

Step 2. *Feel the apparent emotion.* I was as angry as I needed to be, so that was no problem.

Step 3. *What else did I feel?* When Marian first phoned and scolded me I was terribly upset at having hurt her.

Step 4. *What did this remind me of?* No useful ideas came to mind, so I asked myself, *"What do I seem to be doing?"* I tried to take an objective view of my behavior over the past few days. If I were an outsider I might say with Bernie, "What's all the fuss about? You can't stand this woman anyway. Be glad you're getting rid of her. Forget it." This certainly made sense, intellectually. Then why was I having so much trouble? Why was this incident so important?

I went back to Step 3. *What else did I feel?* When Marian phoned me I felt intense *anxiety* about her hurt feelings. I wasn't simply sorry that she was hurt; I felt scared, as if something terrible would happen if I could not prove to her that she was wrong, that I never meant to hurt her. I was frightened long before I thought about her threat to stop my work, but I had not known what I was afraid of. In fact, I realized now, my talk with her superior, while it seemed to settle the real problem, had not calmed me down as I had expected. My apparent feeling now was anger, but I could not stop thinking about her. I was acting *as if* Marian and her feelings were of vital importance to me. Why? What could she do to me? *What did this remind me of?* (Step 4.)

And now I began to re-live an old scene from my childhood that

I had long forgotten. I went back to my nine-year-old self. For two horrible years I had been living in the country under the care of a sadistic foster mother and now my father (who visited weekends) had quarreled with Mrs. J. In his impetuous way, he had packed our bags, phoned for a taxi and now we were at the little railroad station waiting for the train to come and take me away forever. I had never confided the details of this hellish existence to Dad (for irrational reasons which I have only lately begun to understand). So he never knew just why I trembled as I clung to my rescuer's hand and asked fearfully, "What if she catches up with us before the train comes?" My father looked down on me benignly from the Olympian heights of his adult world and laughed. "What are you talking about?"

"If she gets here first she'll take me back." I was rigid with fear. In calm amusement he assured me that Mrs. J. had no such power. He was my father; she was merely a woman he had hired to take care of me. Her authority ended when he broke the contract.

I was not less intelligent than the average nine-year-old, my intellect absorbed what he said, but deep down I did not believe him. Mrs. J. had always seemed like a witch to me. My nine-year-old mind said there are no witches, but on another level I believed she had *magic powers*. I knew Dad could not understand, so I kept quiet, but I was in fear and trembling until we were safely in our seats and I could see the station moving back in the distance. I strained my eyes but no, she was not running after us, so I could breath normally again.

This was the first time I had ever remembered the details of that scene and re-lived it in all its tension and relief. A second later I realized that my anger toward Marian was gone. The whole situation suddenly was trivial; I couldn't have cared less about our misunderstanding.

Step 5. *Look for the pattern.* I saw now, for the first time, that the child within me had gone on believing, ever since I had first become involved with Marian, that like Mrs. J., she too had magic powers. That was the real reason I could never give up: I was afraid of her. That old, sad story about feeling sorry for her, poor lonely creature, was just a cover for my helpless fear. I had been hiding from myself the knowledge that I believed I was in her power. That was why I acted like a friend, why I listened to the venom she poured out day after day even though I writhed. It was that very venom which proved to the child within me she was a witch, like Mrs. J.; it was her evil strength that gave her power over me.

Now at last I was free. I had listened to the child within me and the adult could take over and assert positively that there are no witches. I could get rid of Marian once and for all; and that is what I did. In a few days she felt she had punished me sufficiently and was ready to forgive me and go on where we had left off. She phoned and very sweetly, with no mention of the recent unpleasantness, offered to pick me up and drive me to a meeting. I politely but firmly refused her offer with a suitable excuse. I attended the meeting, smiled and nodded at her in a formal way and pointedly seated myself far away from her. As the days went by, little by little, Marian made further overtures which I had no difficulty calmly rejecting and she finally caught on. I was free from that old bondage.

Now that I had discovered my hidden belief in witches, I could recall other similar relationships with "powerful" women whom I feared and needed to appease: certain school-teachers for instance. I determined to remember this lesson and not be trapped again.

About a year later I came to one of my Good Listeners with an inappropriate reaction to which I could find no clue. "I'm so unhappy about this singing group," I told Hilda. "I love the music, but I have a funny feeling the leader dislikes me. What do you think?" Hilda had attended one meeting. No, she had failed to notice any discrimination against me. "I'd love to go back," I went on, "but the thought of the next meeting gives me a peculiar, shaky feeling. I guess it's anxiety I'm suffering. I keep thinking Julia doesn't really like me."

"Do you like her?"

"No, not exactly. I think I'm a little afraid of her—she's such an aggressive female. I feel as if I have to stay with her group and make her like me."

"Why?"

Suddenly I remembered Marian and my hidden belief in witches. For a moment I was hot with shame, to think that I was still so childish, still suffering from the same foolish disease, the fear of magic. Then my indecision was over. There were other singing groups and I did not have to hang around and torture that child within me who evidently still had not grown up. So I quit that group and solved the problem.

A few years later, a certain Mrs. L. phoned to tell me she had attended one of my lectures. We chatted for a while; she was obviously a brilliant and extremely literate person who not only shared my reading tastes but could recommend some books and authors I had not yet discovered. Then, without any preamble she announced rather smugly that she had been in and out of therapy for years. "I'm not interested in anything you have to teach but I think we have a great deal in common. You seem to be quite intelligent and well-read, so I've decided I'd like to be your friend, not your student." I was taken aback by this brutally direct approach. (Surely friendship is something you kind of sneak up on gradually, not jump into like cold water; and isn't it usually a mutual, unspoken agreement?) But I could not bear to hurt her feelings, so I agreed cautiously that this might be nice, pointing out however that I was very busy and compelled to do most of my visiting on the phone. "Never mind making excuses," she snapped briskly, "if you're too busy too often I shall know you are rejecting me."

Our conversation left me uneasy. I wasn't sure how I could handle this if she became too demanding. She seemed very bright and stimulating, if a little intimidating, but I really was a busy person. I told Bernie about her that night. "Poor thing," I said sadly, "her approach is so eccentric, she must scare people to death. I bet she's always chasing people away and wonders why."

Bernie's response was brief and to the point: "Sounds like a nut. Better keep away from her."

But I kept thinking of all those past rejections and I could not bear to add to them. That phone conversation, with its pitifully childish demand masked by the surface arrogance, haunted me. I did not have time for visiting but I could find an occasional half hour for a telephone friendship of sorts. I had already followed up some of her suggestions and read a few books she recommended, so I called her up to share my ideas with her. We had an interesting chat (she really was unusually clever) and when I hung up I breathed a sigh of relief at having handled this so smoothly.

But my self-congratulations were premature. Next week Mrs. L. phoned to *demand* (that is the only correct word) that I run over to visit her today. It was one of those hectic days when I knew I would be running a race with the clock every minute, but the imperious tone of her voice brooked no refusal. I did not dare put it off for another day. "Well," I faltered, "it's a rough day for me. I may not make it till late in the afternoon," hoping she would get the message and let me off the hook.

"Quite all right," Mrs. L. snapped. "As long as you get here." And that was that. So all day I ran around like a one-armed paper-hanger with the hives, trying desperately to fit that visit into my crowded schedule. Toward evening, when I longed to put my feet up and glance at the newspaper before getting supper ready, I arrived at her house.

What I really needed at that moment was coffee (preferably intravenously) but my hostess forced sherry on me and proceeded to deliver a sophisticated monologue evidently designed to shock me or test me . . . or something. There was no more of our Great Books discussion. Instead, with a kind of hysterical brilliance, and a voice growing gradually shriller and faster, Mrs. L. deliberately flaunted all her personal prejudices and off-beat ideas. I am never shocked by personal revelations when people reveal themselves in real sincerity, although I am frequently moved by their suffering. But this was something very different: a kind of phony naughtiness, an affectation of wickedness, a contrived and self-conscious recital that could only embarrass and, at length bore me. I felt she was trying, in some mysterious fashion, to impress me. Perhaps the combination of sherry and fatigue dulled my wits, but all I could do was smile politely, painfully, and wonder how soon I could gracefully escape. When, after a decent interval I made a rather awkward departure, her farewell words rang ominously in my ear: "Now remember, if I don't hear from you soon I shall know you are rejecting me." It was a form of blackmail I could not resist.

For days I went around worrying about Mrs. L. I could not afford to spend any more time visiting her. Besides, it was only her telephone personality I enjoyed; in the flesh, she terrified me. Should I phone her again? Talk about the new book I had just finished? Explain once again that I only had time for telephone friendships? Apologize for not inviting her over? Bernie was disgusted with me. "For God's sake don't phone her. It'll only encourage her and besides she won't be satisfied with that. Leave her alone."

Intellectually, I knew he was right, but my emotions were pushing me in a different direction. I felt a terrible urge to phone her: I felt so sorry for her, so guilty about rejecting her. I began to realize I was thinking obsessively about Mrs. L. and that was Step 1. *Recognize an inappropriate reaction.* Time to look within and see what I was hiding. So I talked to one of my Good Listeners; not Bernie, he was too full of "good advice" just now to help me use self therapy. I told her all about Mrs. L. from the first phone call through the visit and up to my present preoccupation. "Poor thing," I concluded, "I'm so sorry for her. Sure, she's eccentric. That's just why I hate to hurt her: she must have been hurt so many times." That was Step 2. *Feel the apparent feeling.* I felt pity.

Step 3. *What else did I feel?* How about that very first phone call when she forced her "friendship" on me in that aggressive way? What did I feel then? Just before I began to feel so sorry for Mrs. L. I felt shocked and helpless, as if I were saying, "This woman wants me for a friend, and she is so strong and self-willed that I must do what she wants."

Step 4. *What does this remind me of?* Suddenly I remembered Marian and my hidden feeling that she was a witch with magic powers. "Here I go again," I groaned. "Will I never grow up?" Mrs. L. was another witch for me; the child within me was terrified of her.

Step 5. *Look for the pattern.* I was doing the same thing with Mrs. L. that I had done with Marian: using pity ("She needs me") to cover the hidden fear of her "magic" powers.

Now that I saw the pattern, I was free. Of course it was absurd to phone Mrs. L. and hope to assuage her inordinate demands with a telephone relationship. I could see that now. I knew that I should never have phoned her in the first place: that call led to her invitation. I had gone out of my way to start something I did not want to finish. There was only one way to nip this unfortunate relationship in the bud before it could grow more painful. I did not phone her. Also I resolved to stick to my guns and bravely refuse all her invitations. But it never came to that: when I failed to follow up that visit with any overtures, Mrs. L. took the hint and I never heard from the poor lady again. As for my obsession and guilt, they disappeared as soon as I remembered the old hidden belief in magic and witches.

MARRIAGE: AN AMERICAN FANTASY

WE AMERICANS do not believe in the arranged marriage, an institution primarily designed for bearing and rearing children, the union of two families for the purpose of continuing the family line. Ours is the romantic marriage of love: two young people get together simply for their own sakes. We have made a cult of the pursuit of happiness and we look to marriage to fulfill all our personal needs.

Have you been lonely all your life? You will then expect marriage to provide you with perfect companionship. But ours is not a simple, homogeneous society. In this melting pot each of us has a different heritage and even if you marry the boy next door he is a stranger. His family has old family jokes about things your family holds sacred; he speaks your language but the words have different meanings. It takes a long time for two strangers to become real companions.

Were you a deprived, love-starved child? You will look to your marriage partner for the kind of all-accepting, unconditional love a mother gives her helpless infant. But it takes time to build up the other person's faith in your motives so that he feels perfectly safe. Only after he has learned to trust you completely, to know that you are always on his side, that you will never exploit him can he stop protecting himself and begin to give you some of that unqualified love that comes with perfect security.

The neurotic brings his neurosis to marriage. Nothing is sadder than two dependent people vainly trying to lean on one another, each feeling cheated because marriage has not provided the pillar of strength it promised.

The mass media has led us to believe that marriage is the Happy Ending which solves all problems, but in truth it is only the beginning: it takes hard work to make a good marriage. Too many Americans do not realize it takes time to make a marriage successful, so if their personal problems are not magically solved in short order, then the marriage was "a mistake," they were not really "in love," and they have to shop around for the "real thing." This is especially true when the first sexual excitement wears off. Many a troubled person has what Freud called an incest barrier. That is, the child within him is still fighting the temptation to love (sexually) a member of his original family: only love with a stranger is permitted. But in marriage that stranger eventually becomes a member of the family, the strangeness wears off. Now the loved one is taboo as a sexual object. Coldness, boredom with sex in marriage, is often a cover for that hidden incest taboo. One who suffers from this symptom finds himself easily aroused by a *new* stranger, and then he tells himself that now he is really in love, the other was a mistake. Unfortunate people like this may change partners again and again in a vain, frantic attempt to find that happiness which seems to be just around the corner.

The woman in our culture goes into marriage expecting to find her true identity, to fulfill herself. All her experiences, from early childhood, have conspired to teach her that her main object in life is to get a man. (Be charming, beautiful, poised, intelligent—but not too obviously intelligent—; be a good listener, an entertaining conversationalist, well-groomed, well-read; be up on the latest news, use the right deodorant so He will appreciate you.) She has concentrated so much effort in this direction that she has neglected to develop her true potential, her inner resources. Even if she has begun to prepare for a career it has been with one eye on marriage. She discards her educational ambitions as soon as the Right Man comes along and later is expected to go through a kind of intellectual hibernation while her children are small.

Meanwhile, the mechanics of household living, which her culture has taught her to despise, and which, thanks to modern improvements have become so efficient and automatic as to lose any of the creative aspects they may have had for her great-grandmother (baking bread, clothing the family) bore her to death. Her days are filled with simple, monotonous tasks which demand little of her ingenuity and much of her time, like the "busy-work" assigned by the uninspired teacher, guaranteed to dull the brightest pupil.

She depends on her husband for entertainment and intellectual stimulation. Margaret Mead says that the custom of going steady at an early age leads to unrealistic expectations of marriage. Instead of developing deep friendships with those of their own sex, many girls begin to depend on their boy friends for companionship in play and study. Later, they will expect to share everything with their husbands, but a man who works all day amid the companionship of other men, wants to come home and relax. His wife has been cooped up with small children all day and is starved for adult conversation and a change of scene. The American style of family life isolates each small new family unit. She does not have the help and companionship of other women living in the same house: a mother, sisters, a maiden aunt (or, as in some cultures, other wives!) With an education similar to her husband's and the expectation of a full, exciting life, she suddenly feels trapped, cheated. If she does not use these domestic years to develop her own inner resources, her talents and interests, she may blame her husband for her frustration ("You never take me out.").

Perhaps she will channel her personal drives toward "helping him succeed" as recommended by the slick ladies' magazines. An ambitious woman, craving the vicarious satisfaction of her husband's success to make up for her own vegetable existence, will push him mercilessly. Let us suppose he was one of those unfortunate children who had to buy his parents' love and approval by fulfilling their expectations of accomplishment. He has been led to believe that marriage (the American fantasy) will provide him with the unqualified acceptance he missed in his childhood, that here someone would love him for what he was, not for what he did. Now his wife's attitude pushes him back to his boyhood position. This kind of "help" toward a career can lead to neurotic symptoms, psychosomatic illness and, of course, an unhappy marriage.

Some young women have been so sold on "togetherness" that they deliberately stop themselves from growing emotionally and intellectually. One young mother told me she was exploring books on philosophy and beginning to question some of her old, rather vague ideas. She found this very exciting but she was worried. "I can't share these ideas with John," she sighed. "He thinks it's all nonsense. We went through college together and were so close to one another. I'm afraid to go on in this new direction. I feel disloyal to him. Won't it hurt my marriage if I grow away from him in this way?"

Here was exceptionally bright girl who thought she must stop growing if her marriage partner could not share her new interests. This fear is not only unfounded, but actually the contrary is true. If she shuts a door on her intellectual curiosity she will end up resenting him, blaming him for her boredom and discontent. This kind of martyrdom, this being untrue to oneself, and then passing the buck to the other fellow is what spoils many marriages. When each person

131

can permit himself and the other to develop to the height of his own potential, even if that involves going in slightly different directions, their relationship is enriched by the accumulated new vistas. Each is happier and more fulfilled and so can make the other happier; each respects himself more and is now able to have more respect for the other.

The trouble is young people have been taught that common interests are vital for a good marriage. As a matter of fact, common interests are not too important as long as their basic values are similar. If they cannot agree on right and wrong it will not help them to share the same hobbies.

Traditional attitudes toward money can be a real source of friction for example. If one has been reared in the old-fashioned middle-class virtues and feels wicked buying anything he cannot pay for in hard cash, and the other (in tune with the modern American way of Life) thinks it's smart to buy now, pay later, they are in trouble.

Again, suppose the husband feels a strong responsibility to his fellow-men and the urge to share his earnings with what he considers worthwhile causes. His wife, on the other hand, believes that charity begins (and ends) at home: trouble.

Or perhaps the husband feels that the goal of life is the pursuit of pleasure, and children a mere by-product who should not be permitted to interfere with his freedom. To his wife, the children's needs come first. He wants to keep on the move; she has a deep need to grow roots. Again, trouble.

But if they agree on basic attitudes toward life, a couple can afford to have different interests. Certain concerns they will naturally have in common: their children's welfare, economic and social problems of family life. But the person who is emotionally healthy enough to love another for himself, not merely for the needs he can supply, will be concerned with the other's growth. In this kind of marriage the different intellectual pursuits do not threaten their relationship. They enrich one another's background, adding another dimension to each other's view, just as marriage helps each to understand the opposite sex in ways he could not have learend otherwise.

Here is a sample of the way self therapy can help us escape from some of the accepted myths about marriage. One day a friend loaned me a record album of Theodore Bikel's Yiddish Folk Songs, and I had a wonderful afternoon playing it over and over, recalling bits of that old language I once understood as a small child; I could follow the translation and the transliteration on the cover. Some of the songs were funny and I laughed aloud, some were sad and brought a lump to my throat. I could hardly wait for Bernie to come home that evening: I was so eager to share them with him. Bernie remembers his Yiddish better than I and would be able to appreciate the subtle nuances missed in translation. I looked forward to enjoying his pleasure vicariously.

Like a good wife I wisely refrained from forcing the new album on him the minute he walked in. I admit I enthused about it during supper, but I waited patiently until he finished eating, had stretched out comfortably on the couch and scanned the front page of the evening newspaper before I turned on the record player. Bernie put the paper down and listened politely.

"Isn't he wonderful?" I asked eagerly.

"Very nice." But he didn't laugh as heartily as I had expected at the humorous songs.

"Wait 'till you hear this one" and "The next one is beautiful" I kept saying, but somehow his attention began to wander and after a while I saw that he was absorbed in the newspaper once again. "Don't you want to hear the second side?" I was shocked.

"Well, enough is enough," Bernie said apologetically. "You know I'm not crazy about folk singers.

I knew this was true, and Bikel is not really a singer but a marvellous actor who knows how to put a song over. I was so furious, however, I could have killed Bernie. I did not trust myself to speak for fear I would say too much (when in doubt do nothing), so I left the room as soon as possible to nurse my rage in solitude. But in that brief moment the crazy thought flashed through my mind, "I didn't have to marry a Jew!" That is, what was the point of marrying a fellow-Jew if he wasn't willing to share the language with me?

Now this was really irrational as I recognized even while thinking it. True, my father had warned me all during my youth against marrying outside the faith, but I had not heeded his words too carefully. I had dated non-Jewish boys in my time, and had some serious crushes on some of them. I certainly did not marry Bernie primarily because of his ethnic background. I would have married him if he came from Mars and had green skin.

After a while my anger dissipated, but I knew I had a future assignment: I would have to explore that peculiar unspoken complaint; it was obviously an inappropriate reaction, Step 1.

The next day I spent the afternoon with a friend who is also a good listener. By this time I was feeling kindly toward Bernie, but instead of letting sleeping dogs lie (I knew by now I could not afford that luxury) I deliberately told her, "I had a funny experience yesterday and I'd like to figure it out." I went on to tell her how I felt about Theodore Bikel's Folk Songs. I built up a vivid picture: how I had been waiting all day to share it with Bernie, how frustrating he was, how I felt. Finally I was furious with him all over again. I had arrived at Step 2. *Feel the apparent emotion.*

Step 3. *What else did I feel* just before I became so angry? I remembered how I was just about to turn the record over to side two when I caught sight of Bernie, his nose buried in the evening newspaper. How did I feel? I wasn't really too surprised. Even while he was still listening I sensed he was just being polite. I felt I needed to force him to hear just one more number; I kept hoping that the next song would hit a responsive chord in him. Before the anger took over, I felt less disappointment and surprise than deprivation. I felt cheated, like a child at the mercy of an adult: an adult who refuses to give the child what he needs desperately.

Step 4. *What did this remind me of?* When did I feel cheated in just this way? When was I starved for someone to share my enthusiasms and discoveries? Suddenly I remembered how it felt to be a small girl without a mother: how exciting it was to learn to read —nobody cared; how I brought home my important little projects from school—and nobody looked at them. For a moment I was that little girl again, bursting with enthusiasm, facing the anticlimax of adults who could not share them because they were involved with their own personal lives. I wasn't their little girl. Teacher gave me a gold star? They couldn't care less! That starved feeling hurt more now than it ever did in those early days. I was too busy then, just getting along, to take time to observe just what was wrong. Children are too practical to be philosophers. They avoid feelings and ideas they have not the strength to manage comfortably; they need all their energy to survive in their complicated world.

I was grown up now and could afford to feel, belatedly, the deprivation I took for granted long ago. In a few minutes the deprived feeling was gone and I was my safe, adult self again.

Step 5. *Look for the pattern.* Now I could see what had happened yesterday. More than that, I could look back and recall how many times I had been through this before with Bernie. Like so many people

I had been expecting marriage to undo the past for me, make up for what I had missed. I was expecting Bernie to share all my enthusiasms as a loving mother does for her small child who is just beginning to explore the world around him. She is enchanted with the drawings he brings home from school, proud of his progress in reading and writing; she joyfully follows his intellectual and emotional development.

Now I could recall how difficult it was for me in the first years of our marriage to accept the fact that Bernie would never read novels, how I tried vainly over and over again to share with him my delight in a favorite author, how frustrated I felt each time I failed. Little by little through the years I had learned to recognize the differences in our interests, to appreciate (each time he simplified for me some exciting concept in science or I did the same for him in the humanities) how our very differences enriched one another's lives, added new dimensions to our relationship. So, intellectually, I knew by now that so long as we shared the same basic values and agreed on the important things it was not too vital for him to share my taste for folk music. And yet, every once in a while the child within me demanded a parent to enter into *all* my joys, reflect *all* my tastes. After I had peeled away that layer and caught a glimpse of the deprived, lonely child I used to be, I never again had to hate Bernie for not sharing my hobbies. From time to time I still catch myself trying to coax him to attend some event or read a book that would certainly bore him; then I remember that I am a big girl now: I can see that opera, read that novel without him and then bring back some bits gleaned from the experience that Bernie can enjoy with me in his own way.

HIDDEN ANGER

I HAVE so frequently described anger as a pseudo-emotion, an apparent feeling used to cover other, hidden feelings, that students sometimes ask, "Is anger always an inappropriate reaction? When we're angry does it always mean we're hiding something from ourselves?" The answer is no. There is a time and a place for genuine, appropriate anger. For instance, the civilized person responds to injustice and cruelty with anger. Man is more than just a creature formed by his environment: he is capable of changing his environment too. Healthy anger can motivate him to constructive action that may make his world a better place to live in.

But very often anger is used to cover other feelings, just as it can be hidden by other feelings. Some people use anger as a stereotyped reaction, a handy disguise for different kinds of emotions; they are always ready to fly off the handle. Long ago they discovered that for them anger is less damaging to their self-esteem than helplessness, fear, dependency, anxiety, shame, guilt, etc. The lady in the chapter, "How to Stop Playing Dangerous Games," was this kind of person. She was covering up the fear of rejection with anger, and each day she found something else to be angry about. If you notice yourself getting angry too often at very little provocation, ask yourself if this may be your stereotyped reaction to all kinds of experiences. Look for the next opportunity to explore it: the next time you feel anger treat it like an apparent emotion, use self therapy and see what you are hiding from yourself.

Some people, on the other hand, have a different problem. We are afraid to feel anger and go to great lengths to avoid it. Of course, some of us can easily be furious with our children, but usually at inappropriate times. Children are our natural victims: they keep right on loving us, no matter what.

Just as peptic ulcer is usually caused by hidden dependency (See chapter, "The Hidden Craving for Dependency"), colitis seems to be an illness typical of people with too much hidden anger. The most tragic case I ever read was of a little boy whose mother, over-posses-

136

sive and manipulating, consistently frustrated him under the guise of extreme mother-love. This child, hemmed in every way, prevented from growing and experimenting with life which was his natural birthright, could not afford to hate his mother on whom he was so dependent. He was hospitalized with severe ulcerative colitis, bleeding, wasting away. The prognosis, at the time the case history was written up, was death.

This is an extreme and dramatic story, but many of us suffer various neurotic symptoms because of our hidden anger. See the chapters, "Detective Work in Self Therapy" and "The Meaning of Self Acceptance," for descriptions of how depression and headache can disguise anger.

There is another story like those. I lived in a tract once where my neighbor's living room was too close to my bedroom. We usually retired fairly early and she habitually sat up late watching television. If her window was open we felt as if the TV set was right in the bedroom with us. Besides being bored to tears by her horrible taste in programs, we could not sleep. We were on pretty good terms with her however and if we phoned and cautiously, politely suggested that she close her window she always did so. No problem, you would think.

But strangely enough, every time I lay awake trying to shut out the sounds of that infernal invention, it would take all my courage to go to the phone and make my humble request. Each time I would try to put it off. Maybe she'd think of that open window herself. Maybe she'd grow bored with the dull programs and go to bed. How could she stand it? Didn't she need sleep? Sooner or later I would be driven in desperation to call her and then, from the moment I approached the phone until it was all over, I would suffer all the symptoms of anxiety: palpitations, profuse perspiration, shortness of breath, shaky hands. Later I would breathe a sigh of relief and crawl back into bed as if after a terrible ordeal. When Bernie discovered my problem he offered to phone. But then I lay rigid, listening, trying to put the pieces of the conversation together, and suffering all the same symptoms just as if I were talking to her myself.

One night as I lay there trying to gather strength for the inevitable phone call I began to pay attention to those anxiety symptoms and asked myself, "What am I afraid of?" I did not know. That was Step 1. *Notice an inappropriate reaction.* Was I afraid my neighbor would refuse to cooperate? No, she always closed her window when we asked. And even if she did refuse, so what? What would happen?

I deliberately went to the phone, picked up the receiver, and there was Step 2, *Feel the apparent emotion.* I was terrified without knowing what I was afraid of.

Step 3. *What else did I feel?* Just before I had realized I would have to phone her, what did I feel? Annoyance. Why did we always have to beg her to shut her window? Why did she put us in this awkward position time and time again?

Step 4. *What did this remind me of?* She was so tactless in many ways. You never knew what unpleasant thing she would say or do next, always with that bland smile which took us off guard, as if she were saying, "Who, me? I didn't mean any harm. Don't be a poor sport." All the neighbors were fed up with her and we often wondered whether she was as stupid as she appeared or basically nasty. Was she using that foolish facade to hide her real motives, a disguise to avoid the consequences of her maddening behavior? We had a tendency to say, "Oh, you know Ellen. She's so dopey, you can't take her seriously." I could never be angry with her because I never considered her an equal.

Now I thought to myself, "The trouble with Ellen is she's so unpredictable. I don't really know how she'll react when I phone her. Sometimes she's so sweet about it: "Oh, I didn't realize how late it was. So sorry." But other times she acts as if I'm infringing on her God-given rights. The fifth freedom: freedom to hear television. What about my freedom from television? Don't I have rights too?

Suddenly I felt my hidden feeling: I was afraid she might say something so outrageous that I would be forced to be angry. Since I disliked her so intensely, I felt it would be dangerous to let myself feel true anger toward her: it might be too powerful. Here was an old problem of mine, the fear of anger. I dared to feel that fear for a few seconds and then it was gone. The anxiety symptoms were gone too. I dialed Ellen's number with the clear understanding that she might be in one of her more obnoxious moods and I might have to be angry, but I would take that step when I had to. It would not kill me.

Actually, she was feeling civilized that night, and she graciously condescended to let me go to sleep, so I was spared the anger I dreaded. I never again had to suffer anxiety symptoms when phoning her about television.

About a year later Ellen met me down the block and began sticking verbal pins in me, under the guise of a friendly chat. I was busy reminding myself how silly she was, not to be taken seriously, etc., and kept up a kind of oral ping-pong until I could no longer bear it. Then I came inside and began to tell Bernie about it. "She's so childish! You wouldn't believe it, but you know what she said? . . . and I said . . . and then she said. . . ." On and on I went, rehashing the whole absurd thing in an obsessive way. Suddenly I noticed how shaken I was. "I don't know why I bothered to argue with her," I said.

"I don't know why either," Bernie commented drily.

"And I don't know why I'm so upset. Why do I take her seriously? She's so silly. What's bothering me?" I was having trouble breathing. "What am I afraid to feel?" Suddenly I knew what the feeling was: anger. For the first time I let myself be absolutely furious with that infuriating woman. (Bernie said it was about time, too.) I ranted and raved and recounted all the outrageous things Ellen had said and done in the past, things I had always laughed off. At last I dared to let that accumulated rage out. In a little while I cooled off and felt greatly refreshed. There's nothing like being honest with yourself!

Now I knew what my true feelings about Ellen were: not cool and superior and amused at her childishness, but simply angry. She had been getting away with murder all this time because I was afraid of my hidden anger. Now I was able to handle her in a new way. I could not openly quarrel with her or be obviously rude: but I could, and did, avoid her like the plague. I knew my old weakness, fear of anger, but I was now predictable to myself. This woman would always tempt me to feel anger and I could spare myself that inner conflict by keeping my distance. I carefully and openly kept out of her way, treated her with a studied politeness even she could not fail to understand, and solved that particular problem. One of the great advantages of self-awareness is the new-found ability to avoid aggravating the child within. Why look for trouble?

Sometimes anger can be used as a cover to hide anger. That is, you think you are angry with one person but you are really avoiding anger with someone else. For example, a father may let off steam yelling at his children when he is really furious with his wife; or pick on his wife when he comes home pent-up with rage toward his boss which he has not dared to feel. See the chapter, "How to Feel a Dangerous Emotion," for safe ways to channel anger. Writing is one of the best techniques for this.

139

One day Bernie brought home a lovely little knife with a serrated edge, especially designed for slicing tomatoes. He had noticed it in a store window and could not resist buying for me. I tried to be polite, but I was not grateful and I'm afraid I showed it. Bernie was surprised at my ungracious response and a little hurt, but I could not seem to explain why I was annoyed instead of pleased with this little gift. After a while I noticed that my teeth were aching and I knew I was in for one of my headaches: a clue that I was hiding something from myself. I was suffering from tension but I did not know what my emotion was. This was a good time to use the writing technique, so I shut myself up in my bedroom for a few minutes and this is what I wrote:

"Teeth ache. Beginning headache. Told B. I don't buy what I need. Don't buy kitchen utensils for me. Why not? I don't indulge myself. Don't allow myself luxuries. Why? Feel I can do without unless I can justify purchase by real use. Not a real cook? Like sewing machine? (I had postponed buying a machine for years because I did not enjoy sewing. Eventually bought an old-fashioned second-hand treadle because I was afraid a modern machine would oblige me to do a lot of sewing, and then made all the household drapes, bedspreads and even some dresses for the girls.) Guilty about skills? Inadequate? Ashamed? (Note that all these questions were attempts to bring forth a new emotion. When they failed I veered off to something different.) Don't be "good" to me by doing what you want. You don't understand my needs. Do I feel B was hypocritical in buying impulsively? Didn't understand my needs? Didn't care about my needs? How do I feel? Resentful. Frustrated. If you carelessly buy then it prevents me from buying. Don't "give" thoughtlessly. Better not to give. Felt cheated. False giving leaves me irritable. Angry? Reminds me of Dad. What did he "give" me? Used to act affectionate, arm around me. (At this point I had a vivid picture of myself as a little girl, sitting beside my father on a long, train ride. I had begun to doze and leaned against his shoulder. Then he put his arm around me and I was cramped forward and could not relax.) I was uncomfortable but couldn't afford to show it. Had to be grateful for any show of affection even at inconvenient moments. Releasing tension in jaws now. How did I feel then? Anxious to fool Dad. Wanted him to think I was relaxed. Afraid

140

he would withdraw affection. Starved for affection. Had to be hypocritical in order to get it. Father insensitive. Self-centered. Unimaginative like a child. I was older than him tho' a small child. Missed my childhood. Cheated. Child should be unconscious, careless. Take love for granted not scheme for it. Father is big baby."

That was my hidden feeling: anger toward my father. I only felt it for a few seconds, and then it was gone. The ache in my teeth and jaw was gone too, and I could feel loving toward Bernie again and laugh at my confused feelings about the tomato knife. It is an excellent little tool and I have used it with pleasure ever since.

What about that anger toward my father? As always, with a hidden feeling, that was only the child within me feeling, for a little while, something she dared not feel many years ago. The grown-up woman I now was could feel love and understanding for the father who had tried to do the best he could. The more frequently you permit that angry child within you to come out and feel, the more loving you can be most of the time.

APPENDICES

"THERAPEUTIC TEACHING" appeared in EXPLORATIONS #5, January 1966 and "How to Stop Playing Dangerous Games" in EXPLORATIONS #10, September 1966. At this time the third article, "Communication Workshop with Self Therapy Homework: A Progress Report" has been submitted to the editor and will appear in the near future.

APPENDIX I

THERAPEUTIC TEACHING
By Muriel Schiffman

IT HAS long been assumed that people cannot learn how to modify their self-defeating patterns in an intellectual setting, that only a "therapeutic relationship" provides the opportunity for real change. I have been teaching self-help techniques to adults in a classroom setting for the past decade. Follow-up studies as well as spontaneous feedback from students indicate that class members are learning self therapy (Maslow's term in personal communication) and showing recognizable signs of growth in their daily lives. Anthony Sutich, editor of the Journal of Humanistic Psychology, describes my lecture style as "therapeutic teaching."

I began to evolve my self therapy techniques nineteen years ago in an attempt to rid myself of a recurring brief depression. I accomplished that goal in two years and have been practicing self therapy ever since. Over a period of time I have lost certain neurotic symptoms such as a peptic ulcer syndrome, a cat phobia, compulsive eating, etc. More important, I have developed a spontaneity in interpersonal relations and freedom to fulfill my true potential that has opened up unexpected vistas for me.

My lectures are informal and conversational, delivered in an atmosphere of warmth and humor; students are encouraged to interject

142

comments and questions at any time. I illustrate my theories with concrete anecdotes from my own personal experiences in self therapy.

As in Alcoholics Anonymous and Synanon, students can easily identify with the speaker. I am not an "authority" talking down to them: I have risen from their ranks and can describe how it feels to pull oneself up by one's bootstraps. I dare to talk about my "bad" feelings, so they gather courage to confront such feelings in themselves. I can experience an irrational emotion and yet act in a rational way, I can feel like a child and still behave like an adult: so can they. Every good teaching relationship has an element of transference. In my classroom, Teacher represents the successful person who, though grappling with current problems, does so in a creative way and is able to enjoy a full, rich life. The student borrows Teacher's strength and dares to try new ways of approaching life.

What do I teach? Something like this: Each person has vulnerable areas where, because of his personal history, certain emotions seem too dangerous to feel. Whenever a present situation tempts you to experience that "forbidden" emotion you tend to cover it up with a fake emotion. Each time you hide a feeling from yourself the pseudo-emotion tricks you into acting in a self-defeating way; you are not free to use your intelligence and experience to solve the immediate problem.

Self therapy is a tool to peel away the layer of that misleading cover emotion and feel the genuine one just underneath. You need not understand how you got to be this way (you are not your own psychotherapist); just *feel* the hidden emotion and the whole picture will look different to you. When you dare to experience your true feelings, you see people as they really are rather than as shadows from your past, you hear what they are really saying rather than distort and misinterpret. Once you have felt your hidden emotion, you are free to use your experience and intelligence to solve this problem just as you do others in areas where you are not damaged.

In each lecture I list five steps in self therapy, using them to structure my illustrative examples.

HOW TO FEEL A HIDDEN EMOTION

Step 1. *Recognize an inappropriate reaction.* You notice yourself reacting to some situation with an emotion your intellect tells you is not appropriate: "Why do I feel so hurt? I know he doesn't mean to

143

hurt me." Since any emotion can be used to cover another, and the fake emotion feels just as real as a genuine, appropriate one, it is difficult to recognize an inappropriate reaction while it is going on, especially if you are a beginner in self therapy. This kind of self-awareness comes more easily with hindsight: "I wonder why I was so angry yesterday. She's only a child!"

Depression, anxiety, obsessive thinking can all be called inappropriate reactions since they are not definite emotions, They are always covers for something you are afraid to feel. Tension, headache, physical symptoms of anxiety, like breathing difficulty and palpitations, are all clues that you are hiding something from yourself.

Step 2. *Feel the apparent emotion,* Sometimes you deliberately try to avoid an inappropriate reaction ("It's silly to be hurt; he doesn't mean it.") but you must feel that emotion, no matter how irrational it seems. There is no short cut to the unconscious: you cannot feel a hidden emotion unless you begin with the apparent emotion which covers it.

Sometimes the apparent emotion seems dangerous ("I'm so furious I could kill her—but she's only a baby!"). You need not act out your inappropriate feelings: thoughts and actions are not identical, they can be separated. Your feelings have no magic power to do harm. You can always take your apparent emotion somewhere else: you can talk it out, write it out, lock yourself in the bathroom and cry it out. But do not swallow it down.

If you are trying to explore yesterday's inappropriate reaction, warm up that cooled-off emotion by talking about it to a good listener.

Suppose you are tracking down the hidden feeling behind a headache. Be a detective and work backward, looking for clues. When did this symptom begin? What happened then? How did I feel?

Step 3. *What else did I feel?* Just before the apparent feeling, what other feeling did you have? Not a hidden emotion, but one you felt for a brief moment and paid little attention to at the time, one which was drowned out as soon as the apparent emotion, was over. You may remember that you felt a pang of fear just before the apparent feeling, anger.

Step 4. *What does this remind me of?* When have you reacted this way to a similar situation? What does this make you think of? Have you ever noticed that you have some peculiar attitudes toward this kind of problem?

If this does not evoke a hidden feeling, ask yourself, *What do I*

144

seem to be doing? For a moment, take an objective view. If you were an outsider, observing your behavior in this situation, what would it *look* as if you were doing?

Here in Step 4 your intellect is asking questions, trying to get a rise out of your emotions. You are not looking for an intellectual explanation for your inappropriate reaction; you are not trying to explain the motives for your self-defeating behavior; you are not your own psychotherapist. You are merely trying to *feel* a hidden emotion. Keep trying different ideas until one of them evokes a new emotion. You will know it is a hidden feeling if it displaces the apparent emotion with which you began.

Step 5. *Look for the pattern.* Do not look for your basic personality pattern at this time, nor anything so broad. Just try to find out what happened here. What hidden emotion were you covering up with what apparent one? You are now predictable to yourself; next time you are faced with a similar problem (tempted to feel that forbidden feeling again), if you can remember what just happened you may not have to cover up again with the same old apparent emotion. You will be free to experiment with a new way of handling the problem; you need not act in the old, automatic, self-defeating way. Now that you know your pattern (the tendency to cover this particular hidden feeling with this apparent feeling under this special set of circumstances), you are free to use your intelligence and experience to act at least as wisely as in those undamaged areas where you never had to hide anything from yourself.

Each of my lectures approaches self therapy from a different angle. Here is an example of the way I use personal material to illustrate my method. In a lecture entitled "The Child's Hidden Message," I explain how your own hidden feelings can interfere with family communication.

Whenever you look within and dare to feel your true emotion you will be able to hear your child's message and know how to respond to it. I had this experience. One evening, when the rattling of pots and pans proclaimed the preparation of supper in the kitchen, my daughter yelled from her room, "When do we eat? I'm *starved!*" Since we always eat at the same hour, the unnecessary question sounded to my harried ears like "What's the matter with the service in this lousy hotel?"

Naturally, I shouted right back, "Stop nagging; act your age; come in and help if you're in such a hurry," etc. This exchange rapidly

145

deteriorated to a hysterical duet. Not until the next day did I recall that we had been going through this off and on for years. Then I reflected (as I had also done for years) that the poor kid couldn't help herself, the "strict" schedule laid down by child guidance experts in her infancy made her cry for her bottle the first few weeks of her life, and here she was, still crying. I understood her problem; I had "analyzed" her unconscious motivation long ago. But it had never helped me to handle her and it did not help now. I could not stand her nagging and I did not know how to shut her up. If you generally get along well with your child as I did, and you find yourself stuck with one special problem over and over again, chances are you are hiding something from yourself. I asked myself, "Why am I handling this situation so awkwardly?" That was Step 1, Notice an inappropriate reaction.

Step 2. Feel the apparent emotion. I was calm now, trying to solve yesterday's problem, so I talked it over with a friend who has a teenager of her own and would be interested and sympathetic. In short order I was re-living yesterday's anger in all its intensity.

Step 3. What else did I feel? Now I could recall that when my daughter first began to yell, just before I became so angry, I felt terribly tense: as if she were standing over me with a whip and I had to hurry, hurry! When the anger came, it released the tension.

Step 4. What does this remind me of; I remembered how she used to cry for the bottle. But that intellectual understanding was not enough, I was still angry ("She's a big girl now. How long must she cry for her bottle?").

What else did this remind me of? Food . . . my compulsive eating; my compulsion to feed my family a balanced diet, etc. Then how did I really feel years ago, when my baby had to cry for her bottle because the pediatrician ordered that I feed her every four hours by the clock?

For the first time I tried deliberately to re-live that scene instead of simply intellectualizing about it. In my mind's eye I saw the baby's room, felt myself standing just outside her door, my eye on my watch, waiting for permission to feed her. I remembered how she cried and how I cried along with her: tears of helplessness, frustration, and . . . guilt. That terrible *guilt* swept over me now in a wave so painful that it felt like yesterday's happening, not years ago. The hidden guilt came out and drowned out all the anger. For fifteen years I had

146

blamed the pediatrician for starving my baby: finally, belatedly, I dared to feel the guilt myself.

Step 5. Look for a pattern. The guilt lasted only a few seconds, and then I could see my pattern. Not the whole design of my relationship with this child, simply the pattern that whenever she screams for food, the old hidden guilt is stirred up and threatens to come out and hurt me. First I tense up and rush around frantically to show what a good mother I am; then, when the tension becomes unbearable, I escape into anger. I act out this self-defeating anger, this pseudo-anger, and that encourages her to scream louder. This adds to my hidden guilt which I then cover up with more anger, etc., etc.

Now that I saw my pattern, I was predictable to myself, I could look forward to an opportunity to face this problem again and try to handle it another way. I was not sure yet what I would do next time, but I knew there would be a next time.

Sure enough, about a month later I heard the same old war-cry, "When do we eat? I'm *starved!*" Once again I began to grow tense, but this time, just before the tensions eased into anger, I remembered the hidden guilt. I did not *feel* it again this time: all I did was recall it intellectually. Immediately my tension relaxed and the tone of my child's voice said something quite different to me. Instead of "What's the matter with the service in this lousy hotel?" it sounded more like "Mommy, I'm suffering. Don't you care?"

Of course I cared. Easily, spontaneously, I responded to her hidden message: "Right away, honey. Supper's almost ready." That was all she needed to hear: not another peep out of her.

In addition to my lectures, I am at present experimenting with a variation on the T-Group, a group testing ground for self therapy. Group discussion deals with the here-and-now, members keep alert for inappropriate reactions in themselves which provides them with homework in self therapy. Opportunities for testing out their new self-awareness are provided by ensuing group meetings.

Local psychotherapists who have worked with some of my students tell me that self therapy as learned in the classroom setting seems to be a good preparation for and adjunct to professional therapy.

The author wishes to thank the following people for their help and encouragement: Abraham Maslow, Brandeis University; Anthony Sutich, Journal of Humanistic Psychology; and James Terrill and Robert Spitzer, Mental Research Institute, Palo Alto, California.

147

APPENDIX II

How to Stop Playing
DANGEROUS GAMES
By Muriel Schiffman

IN A former article,* I described my self therapy method. With this method I have evolved some tools for: a) recognizing dangerous games in marriage, b) discovering the hidden reason for playing, and c) changing behavior in a way which allows one's partner room for growth and permits further enrichment of the relationship. In this article I will describe three broad viewpoints from which to examine dangerous games, list definite clues for self-awareness in game-playing, and conclude with a specific technique for stopping the game in a creative, non-damaging way.

THE PARENT-CHILD GAME

I define good adult communication as the ability to express one's true feelings about the other person without either: a) damaging him or b) degrading oneself. For most of us, this is an art to be learned; it is not built into our culture. On the contrary, a dominance-submission theme characterizes most interchanges, especially between intimates.

To borrow Eric Berne's terminology,* A acts like a Parent toward B:

a) *Judgmental, critical, scolding, labeling.* "You are bad, stupid, crazy."

b) *Punishing.* "How dare you criticize me. Now let me tell you about *your* sins."

c) *Degrading.* "I'm not interested in anything you have to say. Nothing you do can possibly move me."

d) *Patronizing, condescending, protective.* "I understand your problem. Never mind, dear, you meant well and that's what counts."

How does B respond to this treatment? He finds it difficult to respond like a self-respecting, non-damaging Adult. An Adult can truthfully say, "When you do that, it makes me feel irritated (an-

---

* "Therapeutic Teaching," in EXPLORATIONS #5. (Appendix I)
* In *Transactional Analysis in Psychotherapy.*

noyed, angry, furious, frightened, anxious, hurt, helpless, inadequate, ashamed, guilty, confused)."

When A acts like a judgmental, punishing, degrading or patronizing Parent, B tends to respond in one of the following ways:

1. The Frightened Child.
    a) *Appeasing.* "I'm so sorry. Forgive me. You are so right and I am all wrong. Please don't be angry. I'll never do it again."
    b) *Lying.* "It was all a mistake. I never meant it that way. You don't understand."
    c) *Pathetic.* "You're so strong and I so weak. Please be kind."
    d) *Blackmailing.* "I'm so sensitive and you're so cruel. I'm getting a headache (depression, heart attack). You're breaking my heart."
    e) *Withdrawal.* "It's no use. I can't talk to you. You wouldn't understand."

2. The Rebellious Adolescent.
    a) *Insolent, rude.* "I'm not interested. Shut up."
    b) *Tough.* "I don't care. I'm not afraid of you."

3. The Judgmental, Patronizing, Punishing, or Degrading Parent. See above. In this case, A, having behaved like a Parent, B disguises the Frightened Child within himself by acting like another, even more threatening Parent. He fools himself and also A, who is tempted to feel like a Frightened Child but quickly covers up by blowing him(her) self up to a bigger and more threatening Parent. This scares B even more, and he, in defense, becomes more Parental, etc., etc.: two fright-. ened Children scaring each other to death by pretending to be Parents, neither permitting the other to act like an Adult.

I have shown how A, acting the Parent, maneuvers B into the role of Child. This system works in both directions. When B acts the Child, he (she) seduces A into the part of Parent. As long as B is the Frightened child, A can be the Good Parent (patronizing, protective) and both appear to be happy; but the success of this marriage is more apparent than real. Sooner or later, B begins to have twinges of discomfort from the babying he has coaxed from A. In this mood he resentfully switches from Frightened Child ("You're so strong and I'm so weak") to Rebellious Adolescent ("Aw, shut up") or Judgmental, Punishing, Degrading Parent.

149

Now A can respond in one of two styles.

1. He becomes the Bad Parent: judgmental, punishing, degrading. B now takes up the job of "grievance collector" (Edmund Bergler's term) and finds reasons to hate A. If both remain too long in this position, the marriage ends in divorce. (Each then marries his (her) opposite number: A finds another Frightened Child, B another Good Parent. Both are happy until the Good Parent in each new marriage is forced into being Bad; then they are back to this position once again.)

An alternative at this point, when A has become the Bad Parent, is for B to retreat to Frightened Child (appeasing, lying, blackmailing, withdrawing) so A is freed to be Good Parent again. Then all is sweetness and light until the next time B gets qualms about his degraded position and needs to rebel.

2. They may switch roles for awhile. A plays Frightened Child to B's Parent until A is strong enough to take over his (her) original Parent role again. B, refreshed by this excursion into rebellion, is ready once again to settle down to the role of Frightened Child and enjoy the benevolence of the Good Parent until his (B's) next spell of uneasiness about his dependent position.

THE HIDDEN CONTRACT

Now let us examine the marriage relationship from another angle. Here is a typical picture. A is volatile, articulate, dramatic, even at times theatrical in expressing emotions. He (she) exploits his (her) apparent feelings to the hilt but is often unaware of his (her) hidden emotions. He (she) marries B, who has the opposite temperament: calm, phlegmatic, stoical, inarticulate, rarely expressing any emotion.

Both A and B have been drawn to one another for reasons they may partially understand. "I married B because he's so even-tempered. My father had a terrible temper." "I was attracted to A because she was so lively."

The hidden, non-verbal marriage contract insures that each will stay pust as he (she) is, but on a conscious level each nags the other to change. A complains bitterly about B's lack of feeling, secretiveness, non-communicativeness, unresponsiveness to A's feelings. But on a hidden level, A fears any change in B and sabotages B's attempts to change in various ways:

a) Drowning B with words. "You never talk to me, I don't know

150

what you're feeling, why don't you tell me your thoughts, I hate the way you sit there looking so smug. . . ." A babbles on and on, and with the torrent of words frustrates B's efforts to get a word in edge-wise.

b) Blackmailing B with suffering. "Since you said that to me, I've had a headache (depression, etc.)."

c) Acting like a Frightened Child. "You're scolding me. You don't love me. You're making me feel terribly guilty (ashamed)." A says this kind of thing before B has had a chance to fully express himself.

d) Acting like a Parent:
    1. Scolding. "What a terrible thing to say. You ought to be ashamed."
    2. Helpful. "You're angry, aren't you? I *know* you're angry. Why won't you admit it? Why can't you be honest with me?" Here A is trying to force B to express a specified emotion on demand. If B follows these directions, he fails to act spontaneously; if he resists this coercion, he retains his original position of silence.

B, too, tries, on a conscious, deliberate level, to change A, while on a hidden level making every effort to keep A the same:

a) Being a wet blanket. "Don't get so excited. Calm down." These comments, delivered at the height of A's intense feeling, have the exact opposite of their declared intent: they either aggravate A's excitement or add further feelings of being misunderstood and squelched, which are expressed with further drama.

b) Trying to ignore A's expressions of emotion. This provokes A to exaggerate and dramatize in order to gain some recognition and response, leading B to withdraw into passivity, which tempts A to be more dramatic, etc., etc., in a vicious circle.

IRRATIONAL AREAS

Each person has certain vulnerable areas where, because of his personal history, he has learned to avoid feeling his true emotion and covers it up with another, false or pseudo-emotion. Whenever you deceive yourself in this way, you tend to act in an inappropriate, self-defeating way. I call these our irrational areas.

The "good" marriage is one where the irrational areas of the partners rarely overlap one another. When you are feeling comfortable and open to your own feelings, you can afford to be accepting of the

151

other fellow's (occasional) irrational behavior, especially if you are very fond of him. His inappropriate behavior does not seem threatening at such times. A husband growls at the children, and his wife thinks, "Poor guy, he's worried about his job." She gets the kids off his back—"Daddy's tired"—and finds some way to comfort him. Even if she does not know about his job problems, she can give him freedom to be irrational, can take it for granted that he has reasons, can respond to his unspoken need for reassurance.

But if she is hiding some feeling from herself—guilt about her own impatience with the children, perhaps, or inadequacy in her role as wife—she will cover up with indignation and anger: "How can you be so unkind to those poor little kids? Don't come home and take out your frustrations on us." The husband will respond with more anger, neither one is aware of his hidden feelings, each responds to the surface, apparent feeling of the other, and the battle is on.

Whenever two people are being irrational (covering up a hidden emotion with an inappropriate, self-defeating, pseudo-emotion) *at the same time*, they fail to communicate. Only when one person is open to his true feelings can he recognize and respond to his partner's hidden message. In the above story, the husband's irritation toward his children covered his hidden feeling of inadequacy about his job. His wife, when she was feeling comfortable, was able to respond intuitively, spontaneously to his hidden message, the need for reassurance.

The "bad" marriage is one where both members have too many irrational areas in common—food, money, sex, work, recreation, authority, etc. For example, food symbolizes love to Mr. C. If his wife has no hidden feelings about food, she enjoys catering to his tastes, comforting him in times of stress with favorite dishes, perhaps a little amused at his overrevaluation of food, but not disturbed by it. However, if she too is irrational about food, the following kind of interchange ensues:

She: "But liver is so good for you." (Look what a *good* wife I am. Don't you appreciate me?)

He, refusing to touch it: "I can't stand liver." (If you really loved me, you would understand how I feel about liver.)

She, tearfully: "Eat just a little bit of it. It's such lovely liver. Why must you be so stubborn?" (If you really loved me, you would love the food I cook.)

Neither can accept the other's irrational behavior; each, deaf to the other's hidden message, can only respond to the surface, apparent feeling of the other; they argue at cross purposes. The husband feels like a helpless Child at the hands of a manipulating parent, The wife feels like a rejected Child whose parent does not appreciate her. Both act like angry Parents.

HOW TO STOP PLAYING DANGEROUS GAMES

Eric Berne shows us how to recognize some of our dangerous games, but he fails to outline a satisfactory way to stop playing. His case histories in *Transactional Analysis in Psychotherapy* imply that when one player becomes aware of the game and deliberately, with no insight into his hidden motives, suddenly stops playing, the other person suffers and the relationship deteriorates. My own observation and experience leads me to believe that when a person says, "I realize I have been playing this game and now I'm going to stop," unless he goes on to explore his unconscious reasons for playing, he merely changes games, gives up an old game for a new one.

The following example of game changing is a hypothetical case, a composite of several I have observed. The wife says, "I'm sick and tired of picking up my husband's dirty clothes wherever he drops them when he gets undressed. Damn him, he treats me like a servant. I realize now that I've been acting like a Parent for years. I nag and scold, but I always end by picking up after him. No wonder he doesn't change: I'm treating him like a Child."

With no attempt to learn anything about her own hidden motives, she proceeds to "stop playing" the game. "I'm fed up," she tells her husband firmly. "From now on, I'm going to leave your dirty clothes where you drop them. I'll wash whatever is in the hamper and that's all. If you don't change your ways you'll find yourself without any clean clothes.

"It worked!" she reports gleefully to me some time later. "Boy, was he shocked when he ran out of clean clothes! He ranted and raved, but I stuck to my guns. Finally, he learned his lesson, and now he puts his dirty clothes in the hamper." But my analysis is that she has switched from one variation of the Parent-Child game to another. She used to be the weak, nagging Parent; now she is the strong, strict Parent. Her husband used to be a naughty Child; now he is a good, obedient Child.

I have been teaching (and practicing for years) a method of game

153

stopping which avoids game switching. In every game, *both* partners are being irrational, both have hidden feelings. If only one member becomes aware of his own irrational reaction and dares to feel his hidden emotion, he is then in the position of the person described above ("Irrational Areas") in the "good" marriage: he can respond to the other's hidden message and stop playing the game. The more frequently he can practice this kind of self awareness and self therapy, the closer his bad marriage comes to being a good one.

When the other person is irrational, it is a waste of time to try to reason with him. Cold logic is not only useless at such a moment, it merely feeds the flame: he tends to distort it and fit it into his own fantasy. If he sees you now as the strong Parent, your cool explanation of his error sounds like criticism, scolding. This not the moment to argue about who is right or wrong. The thing to look for is the hidden meaning underneath the irrational, apparent message. If you are rational yourself at this moment, you intuitively, spontaneously say the "right" thing; you do not play any dangerous games. But if you too are hiding something from yourself, you need to feel your own hidden emotion before you can be open to his hidden message.

When your partner is irrational, how can you know if you are being irrational too? It is so easy to notice when his reactions are inappropriate; how can you diagnose your own? Here are some clues which indicate it is time to examine your own feelings:

a) You are hating the person you love.

b) You are thinking obsessively about what he did or said.

c) Anxiety (afraid but you don't know what you're afraid of).

d) Depression.

e) You can't stand his (her) attitude; it is intolerable to you.

f) You feel an emotion (anger, fear, jealousy, etc.) so intense that you can't bear it.

g) You keep trying to explain, but somehow you cannot communicate; you are up against a stone wall.

h) You react with an inappropriate emotion (the desire to laugh or cry without knowing why).

Any of the above reactions to someone you care for, toward whom you usually feel warm and accepting, indicates you are hiding some other feeling from yourself. As soon as you can feel that hidden emotion, the apparent emotion—(a) through (h) above—will disappear. You will somehow find a way to cope with the situation just as you do at those other moments when you are comfortable and open to your true feelings: you will spontaneously and intuitively respond to the other's hidden message instead of being caught up in the apparent one which is merely a smoke screen.

Here is an example of my own experience in this kind of self therapy. One Sunday I was washing breakfast dishes when I noticed my husband lugging his sailing gear out to the car. "Why are you leaving so early?" I demanded, then glanced at the clock and was appalled to discover it was noon.

"I'm racing today, remember? I have to leave now to be ready at the starting line."

"But you haven't had lunch."

"That's okay. I can skip lunch."

"Oh, why didn't you warn me you wanted to leave so early? I didn't take the butter out of the refrigerator, and now it's too hard to spread. I can't make you a sandwich."

"Never mind, I don't need lunch."

"You can't skip lunch. Suppose the wind dies down? You might be stuck out there all day. How about an apple and a piece of cheese?"

For the first time, a note of irritation crept into his voice. (Until now he had been patiently trudging back and forth to the car, carrying sails, etc., trying to avoid me while I scurried back and forth at his coat-tails.) "No, I've told you before I don't want to handle cheese when I'm working with the sails."

"Then what can I give you?"

"Give me an apple."

"An APPLE?" My voice had become gradually shriller and now it reached a crescendo. "What kind of lunch is an apple? You need something that'll stick to the ribs—protein."

"Okay, okay. Forget it." And off he went to the races with nothing to eat, not even an apple and HE DIDN'T EVEN KISS ME GOOD-BYE! He might be drowned and never see me again. What a way to leave, heartless, cold creature that he was.

I went back to my chores and wept tears of rage into the dish water. How cruel to punish me just because I didn't have his lunch ready. Spiteful thing. He didn't deserve a wife like me who was willing to stay home and drudge while he went off to enjoy himself. (The truth was I had long ago hinted I was terrified of racing and was always relieved when he found someone else to crew for races.) Why

155

couldn't he compromise and take a simple fruit and cheese lunch? He had done it often before when I'd forgotten a sandwich.

Hours went by while my mind went round and round like a broken record, caught up in obsessive anger. At one point I began to analyze *him* (an old defense against feeling one's own emotions). His mother used to coax him to eat food he disliked, always made a fuss about food. Probably my near-hysteria today reminded him of her. But this line of reasoning did not dispel my anger. All I could think was, "But damn it, after all these years he ought to know I'm not his mother!" When you are hiding something from yourself, "understanding" the other person does not help you to accept his feelings.

At long last it dawned on me that this obsessive anger was an indication I needed to use self therapy. And I was hating the person I loved—another clue. That was Step One, *Recognize an Inappropriate Reaction* (see "Therapeutic Teaching," EXPLORATIONS #5). Step Two, *Feel the Apparent Emotion*. That was the anger. (If you are trying to explore yesterday's anger, to discover what was hidden beneath it, you must revive the anger once again, in order to use self therapy. There is no short cut to the unconscious: you must begin by feeling the apparent emotion before you can get down to the hidden one.) Step Three, *What Did I Feel Just Before the Apparent Emotion?* How did I feel when I first noticed my husband getting ready to leave and realized it was lunch time? Anxious, as if something terrible would happen if he missed a meal.

Step Four, *What Does This Remind Me Of?* At this point, you should not try to *understand* what motivated you. You are merely trying on different ideas for size, hoping to find one which will make you *feel* an emotion different from the apparent one. I remembered other times I had forgotten his lunch, how he was willing then to take fruit and cheese. This did not help; it just made me angrier: why was he so stubborn today?

What else did it remind me of? My irrational attitudes about food. I am compulsive about feeding my family the Absolutely Perfect Diet—blackstrap molasses and wheat germ bread.

When you are stuck at Step Four, when no new emotion is evoked, try asking *"What Do I Seem to Be Doing?"* It occurred to me that when my husband goes sailing, I tend to forget to feed him. This is so unlike me. Did I have hidden feelings about his sailing? (This later led to another adventure in self therapy which was very fruitful.)

If I were an outsider now, observing my behavior, what would I expect a food-oriented person like me to feel when she deprives her husband of a meal? Guilt? GUILT! Yes, that was the hidden feeling. It swept over me like a wave for a few seconds, and then it was gone, and the anger, the apparent feeling with which I had begun, was gone too. A hidden emotion does not last long, although it may be very painful, and it always displaces the apparent emotion.

Step Five, *Look for the Pattern*. I could now see that whenever I deprived my husband of food, I was tempted to feel guilt, and I covered up that hidden guilt with pseudo-anger. When you have discovered a pattern like this, you have no assurance that it will not recur, but forewarned is forearmed. You can do something to help yourself now.

That night I told him I was sorry I forgot his lunch, that my anger was a cover for guilt. "I don't blame you for being angry with me," I said. "I was so frantic and irrational."

"But I wasn't angry," he protested.

"You dashed off without kissing me goodbye."

"*You* were so angry I didn't dare try to kiss you."

"You punished me: you wouldn't even take an apple."

"I asked you for an apple. You wouldn't give it to me."

Now I could see the picture clearly. I had been feeling like a punished, rejected Child, but I sounded like a punishing, rejecting Parent to him. He withdraws when I get too frantic about feeding him; I push further. We are both irrational in this area.

I could predict that I might forget his lunch again and once more cover up my guilt with anger. "Please, next time you race, tell me the exact time you intend to leave the house so I can plan in advance."

Bernie protested that I needn't worry about it nor feel guilt, as it did not bother him at all to miss lunch.

"But it bothers me," I explained. "Please help me avoid that situation again."

He promised he would, and sometimes he did; but somehow, having explored that hidden guilt, I never had to use that pseudo-anger again. The next time he forgot to tell me, I realized I could melt the butter on the stove and paint it on the sandwich with a pastry brush. A simple solution, but one I could not think of when I was busy hiding guilt from myself; we always act in self-defeating ways when we are not open to our true feelings.

What about Jane in the earlier story? Suppose, after she had real-

157

ized the nagging and picking up of her husband's dirty clothes was a game, she used self therapy. The apparent emotion she felt was anger: "Damn him! He treats me like a servant." She might have been able to relive some significant childhood experience and feel a hidden feeling of hurt or degradation. Her apparent anger toward her husband would disappear and the picture would look different. She would find a new way to solve the problem. Perhaps when her husband stopped seeing her as an angry Parent he would become more coopera- tive. Or perhaps she would feel differently about picking up his clothes. Many married people feel perfectly comfortable and self- respecting while performing menial tasks for one another.

When you are hiding something from yourself, you tend to distort experience. Once you have dared to feel your hidden emotion, you can hear what people are really saying; you can see them as their own unique selves instead of as merely shadows from the past. You can stop playing dangerous games.

APPENDIX III

COMMUNICATION WORKSHOP WITH SELF THERAPY HOMEWORK: A PROGRESS REPORT

By Muriel Schiffman

ALTHOUGH I have led fifteen Communication Workshops each group meeting teaches me something new, so I can only refer to this paper as a progress report. I will discuss why people fail to communicate and how they can learn to do so.

WHY WE FAIL TO COMMUNICATE

The American preoccupation with "togetherness" and our easy camaraderie, more apparent than real, thinly disguise our alienation and isolation in the lonely crowd. We have learned to use language to camouflage rather than to communicate our true feelings to one another. Why can't we communicate?

In my Workshops I see people falling into two broad categories in respect to their basic orientation to life, based on their personal his- tories.

I. *The person who sells his soul for love.* He presents an idealized picture of himself to the world in a desperate attempt to win the love and approval he craves. He carefully screens out expression of any feeling or thought that might conflict with this image: he lives a lie. Tragically, his secret fear, "What if they knew the Real Me?", negates any reassurance he may win from popularity, admiration or love.

II. *The person who distrusts the world.* He experiences people as hostile and the world as a dangerous place. He wards off intimacy with apparent indifference and coldness and rarely expresses any emotion. His underlying motive is the fear of being hurt; he pays the price of self-imposed loneliness which serves to reenforce his mistrust of the mysterious other.

In a former article, "How to Stop Playing Dangerous Games" (EXPLORATIONS #10) I described two kinds of personal style in communication: (A) ways we manipulate others (the Parent-Child game) and (B) audience awareness (dramatic-phlegmatic contract). I will now subsume these styles under the basic headings described above.

I. *The person who sells his soul for love.*

A. The Child who seduces the other into the Parent role. When you are acting in the Child mode you appease, lie, blackmail, rebel, or withdraw.

B. The dramatic type who overacts his emotions in a frantic attempt to gain recognition, but tends to arouse distrust in his opposite number (II. B below).

While apparently begging for a response, he shuts his opposite number up by drowning him with words.

II. *The person who distrusts the world.*

A. The Parent who forces the other into the Child role. When you are acting in the Parent mode you condescend, patronize, punish, scold, frighten, interpret, judge, or degrade.

B. The phlegmatic type who is distrustful of the dramatic type and who rarely expresses feelings.

STRUCTURE OF THE COMMUNICATION
WORKSHOP

Sixteen people meet fifteen times in a weekly two-hour session. A nucleus of these members tend to stay together in two or more successive Workshops, with new people filling in at the beginning of the next fifteen-meeting term.

PHYSICAL STRUCTURE

The group is heterogeneous: men and women, opposite types (in terms of the categories described above), different cultural and ethnic backgrounds; marriage partners and parents and offspring are separated from one another in different groups. Each group member tends to find his opposite number and is naturally provoked into acting out some of his self-defeating life patterns. When he discovers himself playing the same "dangerous game" with a stranger that he plays outside in "real" life he develops a self awareness essential for change.

STRUCTURE OF VERBAL INTERACTION

Unlike the T-Group or Encounter Group free talk, Communication Workshop discussion is clearly defined and delimited at the first meeting. Members are told to try to deal exclusively with *one another;* intellectual and philosophic discussions, personal problems dealing with people outside the group, interpreting ("playing psychiatrist"), while not expressly forbidden, are actively discouraged at the start. In short order the members police one another by openly expressing boredom or irritation whenever the talk gets too far away from them, whenever they feel a lack of involvement. They learn to recognize when such "outside" talk is a maneuver to avoid an immediate situation. Printed instruction for Workshop members:

The goal of the Workshop is to learn how to tell another how he makes you feel without degrading him or yourself. When you reach that goal you will no longer need the Workshop. Meanwhile, pay attention to all your feelings here and talk about them: "I feel irritated, annoyed, angry, hurt, frightened, anxious, bored, ashamed, guilty, sad, happy, warm, protective." Do not wait for a dramatic, "important" emotion. Report small feelings of annoyance, restlessness; when someone else describes a feeling you are

160

having, say, "Me too." If you are afraid of sounding foolish, talk about that. Be as spontaneous as possible. The way to learn good communication is to make mistakes in group.

SELF THERAPY HOMEWORK

Unlike the T-Group, designed to provide an experience for un-self-conscious growth, the Communication Workshop, an outgrowth of teaching self therapy (see "Therapeutic Teaching," EXPLORATIONS #5), is based on the assumption that the individual can accept conscious responsibility for his emotional development. Members are instructed:

When a Workshop member gives you negative feedback, tell him how you feel about what *he is doing to you* at that moment (hurt, angry, ashamed); then discuss how you feel about the criticism itself. Do not be in a hurry to change merely to please the group. Instead, take these feelings home and try to use them for self therapy. (Why am I so sensitive to John? Who does he remind me of? When have I felt this way before?) When you are criticized for behavior in the Workshop, try to notice how widespread this behavior is in your "real" life; only then can you decide whether or not you want to experiment with new patterns of behavior.

Be as spontaneous as possible in the Workshop; then later ask yourself if you are really communicating or just "acting out." Communicating is telling how you feel. Acting out is trying to *force* the other person to do something, trying to control his behavior instead of telling him how his behavior affects you. You *must* act out in group, otherwise you cannot learn anything about yourself. Try to observe yourself *after* you act out so you can learn to label it for yourself. Pay attention to what your behavior is doing to the other person. Try to use self therapy to discover what hidden meaning this pattern has for you: it once had survival value for you, although it is self-defeating in your present day life,

A prerequisite for Workshop membership is attendance at my Self Therapy lectures frequently enough to learn self therapy techniques.

ROLE OF THE LEADER

As a leader, I am a strong, supportive authority figure, primarily a teacher. Occasionally I act as a model for the group, responding on a feeling level to a student's behavior when such a response is therapeutic for the student. Instructions:

> Keep a weekly Journal and mail it to me before the next meeting. Write about feelings you failed to express in group, self therapy attempts, any personal information which can help me know you. In this Workshop say whatever comes to mind. Do not censor your words in hopes of saying it the "right" way. The things people say in group are the raw materials I need for teaching and you need for learning.

I use the encounters in group to illustrate my theories of failures in communication, helping the members involved to discover another way the problem might have been handled as in family therapy. I try to wait until all emotional response has been expressed, often until the following week to avoid shutting off emotions with intellectualization. Many students work through their problems with authority figures by feeling negative emotions toward me for a while—fear, anger, suspicion, jealousy. I avoid using material for teaching when it involves a student going through such a phase. Students are encouraged to express their negative feelings toward me so they can have the experience of doing so without being punished, rejected, made to feel guilty or ashamed. This appears to be a therapeutic experience necessary for some people before they can move on to interaction with other members.

ENRICHMENT OF WORKSHOP EXPERIENCE

The Tape. Each meeting is taped and members are encouraged to borrow tapes. Some people are able to feel, belatedly, an emotion in the privacy of their homes they could not experience in the group. They have a second chance to respond to others' comments. Some students who could only say, "I was angry with you at home when I heard you on the tape," eventually learn to feel spontaneously at the appropriate time in the Workshop.

Another learning experience: "I was horrified when I heard myself on tape. No wonder the group was angry. I had no idea I was doing that to people."

Social period. Members are supposed to meet socially after each weekly session (without the leader) in a restaurant or member's home. This develops another facet to member interaction, inspired by the Synanon experience: people who have to get along with one another in a "real" life setting can meet in special sessions to express grievances and clear the air. ("I felt left out at coffee." "You hurt my feelings." "I was angry when you said that.")

THE THERAPEUTIC ENVIRONMENT

The Communication Workshop is a laboratory where the student can act out his self-defeating patterns of behavior, safe in the knowledge that the teacher will intervene when necessary to save the victim from too much pain, the aggressor from too much guilt. This protection of a strong, authority figure who makes demands for conscious work and growth attempts on the part of students, speeds up the period necessary for establishing a "family" feeling. Again I draw on the Synanon literature for the rationale of this therapeutic environment. (See Caserel's theory in SO FAIR A HOUSE: THE STORY OF SYNANON.)

In order to communicate on an Adult level (self-respecting, non-degrading) each person needs the experience of safely performing the developmental tasks of life. Most people were cheated along the way: because of their personal histories some passed through certain stages too quickly, others skipped over or never reached an important stage. The Workshop provides a safe place to live through some of these stages: it gives people a second chance.

In order to gain the emotional rewards of the various developmental stages in life people need to actually live through the experiences which belong to them. There is no short cut: it is not enough to *understand* what we have missed. We must be involved with others and feel and express some of the emotions appropriate to that experience. Each of us must successfully pass through our psychological Childhood and Adolescence before reaching Adulthood. The emotional tasks of each stage:

Childhood. To trust another person and feel safe enough to reveal fear and helplessness to him. To dare to lean on him in moments of weakness without feeling degraded. To accept help.

Adolescence. To express anger openly, even at times when you suspect it may not be completely appropriate. To criticize an authority figure when you think he is wrong. To experiment with new ways of behaving at the risk of being wrong or appearing foolish, and of losing love and approval. To try to communicate with strangers who do not understand you and whom you do not understand.

Adulthood. To accept responsibility for your own errors and try again. To face openly your own guilt, shame, uncertainty instead of avoiding them or blaming another. To tell, when necessary, your true feelings to another without degrading him or yourself.

The Communication Workshop is designed to provide an opportunity for living through the stages missed in "real" life. I am satisfied that some people have been able to make use of this opportunity and have shown visible signs of growth.

HOW WE SHUT PEOPLE UP

Communication is a two-way affair. Besides expressing our feelings to others, we must permit others to express their feelings to us. Here are some ways I see people in the Workshops shutting others up, stopping communication:

1. Explaining too soon; justifying oneself *before* responding to the other's feeling. (The hidden message: You have no right to feel that way.)
2. Reassuring before responding to feeling: "You don't have to be hurt." (You're stupid to feel that way.)
3. Condescending: "Tell me all about it. I want to help you." (I don't care how you feel about me; you cannot move me, I'm so strong and you're so weak.)
4. Blackmailing: "You're giving me a headache, heart attack, depression." (I'm so sensitive and you are a brute.)
5. Responding too soon: "I'm sorry, I didn't mean it, I know how you feel" before the other has had a chance to express his feelings fully. (I don't want to hear. Please stop feeling.)
6. Interpreting: "You are hostile to me because I remind you of your mother." (I don't care how you feel about me; you cannot move me. I'm so clever and you are so sick.)

7. Punishing: "Oh yeah? Well let me tell you what *you* did." (I'll get you, you dirty rat. You'll be sorry you picked on me.)

8. Pretending to be stupid: "Sorry, I don't understand what you're talking about," (and I don't want to, so why don't you give up?)

9. Passing the buck: "That's your problem." (I don't care how you feel about me and you cannot move me. I'm so healthy and you are so sick.)

10. Changing the subject by replying to the *content* instead of the emotion; getting into an intellectual discussion to avoid responding to the other's feeling: "That's very interesting. I've often noticed that women tend to have that attitude toward men. Why do you suppose that is?" (As an individual person you are unimportant. Don't take yourself so seriously.)

11. Playing lawyer: "When did I say that? I never said those words." (You made a mistake in this detail and that proves you have no right to your feelings.)

12. Turning the whole thing into a joke with a witty remark. (You are not worth taking seriously.)

13. Scolding: "That's very rude." (You are a vulgar child, beneath my notice. I cannot take your feelings seriously. You are worthless.)

14. Being bored or absent-minded: "Sorry, I didn't hear you. My mind wandered." (Your feelings are unimportant.)

15. Dead pan, no response. (You are beneath my notice.)

How we stop an encounter between others:

1. Interrupt with your own irrelevant feelings: "That reminds me of what happened to me." (I'm not interested in you people. Shut up and listen to me.)

2. Interrupt with your own relevant feelings before they have had time to express their feelings: "This is upsetting me."

3. Scold the aggressor before the victim has had a chance to defend himself.

4. Express your empathy with the victim before he has had a chance to express his own feelings.

5. Change the subject too soon, before the people in the encounter have had a chance to explore their feelings sufficiently.

6. Express boredom.

One who stops the encounters of others is sometimes afraid of witnessing strong emotions because of his own personal history. He may have been the child who felt responsible for settling his parents' quarrels. He is still trying to avoid that old feeling of helplessness by trying to control the others' behavior.

Shutting the other up is always an attempt at control, warding off a painful experience.

This list, like the article itself, is incomplete—a report of work in progress.